An essay on the use of lights by sea-going vessels : and the rule of the road at sea : with numerous cases and an appendix, containing foreign ordinances, with translations.

Frederic Thomas Pratt

An essay on the use of lights by sea-going vessels : and the rule of the road at sea : with numerous cases and an appendix, containing foreign ordinances, with translations.
Pratt, Frederic Thomas
collection ID ocm32555090
Reproduction from Yale Law School Library
Includes index.
London : Benning, 1857.
vii, 167 p. ; 23 cm.

The Making of Modern Law collection of legal archives constitutes a genuine revolution in historical legal research because it opens up a wealth of rare and previously inaccessible sources in legal, constitutional, administrative, political, cultural, intellectual, and social history. This unique collection consists of three extensive archives that provide insight into more than 300 years of American and British history. These collections include:

Legal Treatises, 1800-1926: over 20,000 legal treatises provide a comprehensive collection in legal history, business and economics, politics and government.

Trials, 1600-1926: nearly 10,000 titles reveal the drama of famous, infamous, and obscure courtroom cases in America and the British Empire across three centuries.

Primary Sources, 1620-1926: includes reports, statutes and regulations in American history, including early state codes, municipal ordinances, constitutional conventions and compilations, and law dictionaries.

These archives provide a unique research tool for tracking the development of our modern legal system and how it has affected our culture, government, business – nearly every aspect of our everyday life. For the first time, these high-quality digital scans of original works are available via print-on-demand, making them readily accessible to libraries, students, independent scholars, and readers of all ages.

The BiblioLife Network

This project was made possible in part by the BiblioLife Network (BLN), a project aimed at addressing some of the huge challenges facing book preservationists around the world. The BLN includes libraries, library networks, archives, subject matter experts, online communities and library service providers. We believe every book ever published should be available as a high-quality print reproduction; printed on-demand anywhere in the world. This insures the ongoing accessibility of the content and helps generate sustainable revenue for the libraries and organizations that work to preserve these important materials.

The following book is in the "public domain" and represents an authentic reproduction of the text as printed by the original publisher. While we have attempted to accurately maintain the integrity of the original work, there are sometimes problems with the original work or the micro-film from which the books were digitized. This can result in minor errors in reproduction. Possible imperfections include missing and blurred pages, poor pictures, markings and other reproduction issues beyond our control. Because this work is culturally important, we have made it available as part of our commitment to protecting, preserving, and promoting the world's literature.

GUIDE TO FOLD-OUTS MAPS and OVERSIZED IMAGES

The book you are reading was digitized from microfilm captured over the past thirty to forty years. Years after the creation of the original microfilm, the book was converted to digital files and made available in an online database.

In an online database, page images do not need to conform to the size restrictions found in a printed book. When converting these images back into a printed bound book, the page sizes are standardized in ways that maintain the detail of the original. For large images, such as fold-out maps, the original page image is split into two or more pages

Guidelines used to determine how to split the page image follows:

- Some images are split vertically; large images require vertical and horizontal splits.
- For horizontal splits, the content is split left to right.
- For vertical splits, the content is split from top to bottom.
- For both vertical and horizontal splits, the image is processed from top left to bottom right.

*Vernon Lushington,
Inner Temple, Nov. 27, 1857.*

AN ESSAY

ON THE USE OF SHIP LIGHTS,

AND

THE RULE OF THE ROAD AT SEA.

AN ESSAY

ON

THE USE OF LIGHTS

BY SEA-GOING VESSELS:

AND

THE RULE OF THE ROAD AT SEA:

With Numerous Cases:

AND

AN APPENDIX,

CONTAINING FOREIGN ORDINANCES, WITH TRANSLATIONS.

BY

FREDERIC THOMAS PRATT, D.C.L.,

ADVOCATE, DOCTORS' COMMONS.

LONDON·
BENNING & CO., 43, FLEET STREET.
1867.

T
P8884
1857

WILLIAM HENRY COX,
5, Great Queen Street, Lincoln's Inn Fields.

TABLE OF CASES.

Independently of the more usual Reports, the Author has availed himself of the full and accurate ones of Cases relating to Shipping given in the "Shipping and Mercantile Gazette"

A

Activ, 73, 129
Adonis, 50
Adventure, 114, 29, 80
Africa, 91
Alexandre, 118
Aline, 98
Aliwal, 52
Anna, 73
Argo, 30, 37
Athol, 8, 105

B

Baron Holberg, 101
Batavier, 86
Beaver, 82
Benares, 9, 62, 105
Berbice, 125
Bessie, 45, 62
Blenheim, 92
Boreas, 43
Borussia, 74

C.

Catherine, 90

Celt, 102
Ceres, 117
Christiania, 73, 89
City of London, 93
Clarence, 36
Cleopatra, 119
Clyde, 11, 34, 46, 65
Colonia, 102
Columbine, 10
Cyrus, 91, 93

D

Dixon v Clement, 55
Don v Lipman, 72
Dumfries, 68

E.

Earl Bathurst, 84
Edward, 107
Effort, 118
Elizabeth Mary Ann, 95
England, 97
Eolides, 65, 80
Ericson, 36, 68, 120
Ernest, 89

F

Fairy, 8, 52
Finland, 103
Fortitude, 105, 106

G

Gorge, 99
Gipsey King, 87, 100
Girolamo, 90
Gloria Deo, 35
Grace Darling, 124
Gulnare, 59

H

Harlequin, 81, 86
Harriette, 31
Hebe, 80

I

Immaganda, 102
Imperatriz, 35
Inflexible, 123
Iron Duke, 3, 10

J.

James, 121
James Holmes, 122
Johan Friedrick, 66
John Biddle, 101
John Sugars, 107
Joseph Somes, 125
Juliana, 56
Jupiter, 98

K.

Kingston by Sea, 95

Kong Hakon, 118
Kron Prins Ernst, 62

L

Legatus, 49
Lidskjalf, 90
Linda Flor, 129
Loftus, 127
Londonderry, 4, 11
Louise, 44

M

Mariner, 94
Mangerton, 60
Mary Maria, 96
Moro Castle, 45

N.

Napoleon III, 33
Neptune, 58, 126
IX Martz, 65, 101
Northampton, 88
Norval, 119

O

Oratava, 8
Osmanli, 7, 11

P

Panther, 42
Presto, 94

Q

Queen Dowager, 58

TABLE OF CASES.

R.

Red Jacket, 103
Reliance, 97
Rival, 129
Rob Roy, 39
Robert Watson, 69
Rose, 2
Royal Consort, 95

S

St. Columbo, 84
Sarah, 6
Sea Park, 100
Seringapatam,
Shannon, 128
Silloth, 127
Sir George Seymour, 101
Sir Thomas Stanley, 92
Six, 91
Smith v Condry, 72
Southampton, 96
Spray, 89
Stadacona, 9, 106
Stranger, 100
Superior, 107
Swanland, 40, 62
Swea, 6
Sylph, 123
Sylph, 41

T.

Telegraph, 30, 46, 53
Telegraph, 38
Temiscouata, 55, 83
Teresita, 94
Test, 99
Traveller, 106
Trident, 44
Troubadour, 87
Two Friends, 63
Two Sisters, 96

U.

Undine, 128

V

Vernon, 66
Vesta, 92
Victoria, 5
Vivid, 32, 47
Volcano, 81

W

Whittle v Crawford, 49
Woodrop Sims, 104

Z

Zollverein, 69

USE OF LIGHTS

BY

SEA-GOING VESSELS.

ONE of the most obvious means of pointing out, during the night and in foggy weather, the position of a body, and guarding against a collision with it, is evidently that of attaching to some part of it lights of such a power, and in such a manner, that they may be visible to some considerable distance from all points around it.

This method, however, of guarding against accident does not appear either to have been ever generally adopted in former times, or to have been introduced amongst those rules which have been gradually established to regulate the navigation of ships, and admitted as applicable to vessels of all nations. This may, perhaps, be partly accounted for by the employment of lights as signals of distress, and notices when the services of pilots are required, as also because, as long as the moving power of vessels passing over the deep was only that of the wind, the practised eye of the seaman was, under ordinary circumstances, able to detect in time any vessel approaching or being approached, provided a good look-out were kept

Since, however, the introduction of steam, the rapidity of movement acquired by the assistance of this power, and the advantages that vessels under its influence possess over those which are still dependent upon sails alone, have induced the legislature of our own and other countries to lay down certain rules, and establish certain regulations for the purpose of guarding against the increasing probability of collision at sea. Amongst these an important place must be allotted to those relating to the use of lights

The subject admits of a twofold division

1. With reference to the use of constant or fixed lights
2. To the duty and necessity of exhibiting or hoisting lights on any accidental emergency

It will be desirable, in the examination of it, to consider what was the state of the law relating to the use of lights by vessels at sea in former times, previous to the introduction of direct legislation on that subject;

What has been the effect of the additional obligations imposed by the legislature;

And what the actual state of the law now is.

WITH REFERENCE to the period preceding legislation, it may be observed that the Court of Admiralty, assisted by Trinity Masters, had during that time, on several occasions, laid it down that <u>no general obligation is imposed upon a merchant vessel to exhibit lights for the purpose of pointing out its position, although, from the peculiar circumstances of a particular case, it may have been its duty so to do upon that occasion, and a neglect in that respect might, in case of collision, deprive the complainant of the right of recovering compensation for injury sustained thereby</u>

ACCORDING TO the preceding division, we have to consider,

1, CONSTANT OR FIXED LIGHTS

2 Ca 101.
Jan 24,
1843.

The law relating to these was fully discussed in the case of the *Rose*

This was a case of collision between the *Rose*, a steamer, and the schooner *Regina*, which occurred in the British Channel, on the night of the 5th October, 1852.

It was admitted on behalf of the *Rose*, that she was proceeding down the Bristol Channel at the rate of 10 knots an hour.

It appeared also from the evidence, that there was a considerable thick haze hanging on the water, so that it was difficult to discover vessels at all, and that none could be seen at a greater distance than a quarter of a mile.

The *Rose* carried three strong lights, the *Regina* showed none.

On the part of the *Rose* it was contended that the *Regina* was in fault, because she carried no lights.

In reference to which, the Court observed that that point had been discussed over and over again for twenty-five years, that the Trinity Masters had always refused to lay down any rule obliging merchant vessels constantly to carry lights, though under certain circumstances it may or may not be right to do so, and this would in each case be a point for the consideration of the Court.

In the subsequent case of the *Iron Duke*, the action was brought against that vessel, a steamer, by the owners of the *Parana*, a brig, which was lost in consequence of a collision which took place between them off the Welsh Coast, on the 10th September, 1844, about 2 o'clock A.M.

The night, according to the balance of evidence, was dark, and the *Parana*, it appeared, carried no light. This neglect, it was contended on the part of the *Iron Duke* was the cause of the accident.

The Court observed that the preliminary[1] question being whether the *Parana* did what she ought to have done, the first inquiry will be this—whether she ought to have carried a light? and referring to the case of the *Rose* before cited, observed that the question whether merchant vessels ought generally or constantly to carry lights or not, was one that had undergone perhaps more examination than any other similar point, the final decision being that there was no such obligation upon them.

And this was confirmed by the opinion *then* expressed by the Trinity Masters, that sailing vessels do not and are not, under common circumstances, required to show a light; the reason being that the showing a light is the signal for a pilot, as was more fully explained in the case of the *Londonderry*

Londonderry

4 Ca xlvi

This was originally a case of collision between that vessel, a steamer, and the schooner *Dolbadarn Castle*, which was tried before the High Court of Admiralty in Ireland, and thence appealed to the Irish Court of Delegates

That Court in giving judgment on the appeal observed, that it appeared clearly that by the rules of navigation it was not incumbent on a sailing vessel to have a light, sup-

---

[1] With respect to proceedings to recover damages for injury caused by collision, it is to be observed that the Court of Admiralty and the Common Law Courts have concurrent jurisdiction in this matter, but this difference is to be noticed between them In the Common Law Courts, the plaintiff will not be entitled to receive *anything* unless he prove himself to be entirely free from blame. In the Court of Admiralty, however, on the part of the vessel proceeding against the other, it must be proved that she was free from blame to entitle her to a complete decision in her favour but if it should appear that both vessels are in fault, the amounts of the damage sustained by each are added together, and each is condemned to pay half of the whole amount, although that half may, and in almost all cases will, exceed the damage one of them has sustained

posing it not to be at anchor with its sails furled, and that because the exhibition of such a light is considered a signal for a pilot.

THE SAME ABSENCE of obligation to exhibit a constan light, extends to the case of vessels at anchor, although it is generally the practice to have a fixed light displayed by them when in that situation. This practice has probably arisen from the peculiar circumstances of the locality in which vessels generally take up such a position, or from the circumstances that such a step is frequently enjoined as a measure of safety and precaution in the rules and regulations laid down by the proper authorities for observance in many anchor grounds *Vessels at anchor*

The leading case on this point, and in which the question was fully discussed, was that of the *Victoria*, in which the owners of the *Three Betseys* proceeded against the *Victoria*, on account of a collision between them, which occurred in the *West Swin*, on the 9th January, 1848, about 2.30 A.M *6 Ca 178.*

The morning was dark, the wind blowing strongly from the *East* Both vessels were on their voyage from the North to London, the *Victoria* proceeding at the rate of six knots an hour, the *Three Betseys* was at anchor

The preliminary and main question in the case, viz, whether this latter vessel was to blame, depended upon this circumstance—whether it was her duty to have had a light hoisted at the time?

The Court upon this point, observed,

The simple question is, What is the rule when a merchant vessel is lying at anchor? whether she is bound or not always to exhibit a light? It is, I apprehend, as settled as any point can be, that there is no such general obligation; but though there is no general obligation, it is equally settled that circumstances may exist in which it would become obligatory on the master of a merchant vessel, to exhibit a light for his own safety, and for that of other vessels, and that upon the simple ground that all persons are bound to take due and proper care to avoid accident. Either by land or by sea, no man can complain of an accident that happens to himself, if by reasonable and proper precautions he could have prevented it

The Court, after consulting the Trinity Masters, expressed its opinion that in this case there was no effective light on board the *Three Betseys*; that looking at the circumstances of the case, the period of the year, the state of the night, and the number of vessels likely to be in the neighbourhood, it was her duty to have had a light burning In that duty she failed, and, not having taken every reasonable precaution, she was to blame

The Court also expressed its opinion that the *Victoria* was to blame for proceeding, under all the circumstances of the case, at the speed at which she was going, and, as both vessels were thus in fault, decreed the damages to be divided between them

Swea,
4 Ca 97

The previous case of the *Swea*, which was one in which that vessel, a Swedish barque, had come into collision with the British schooner the *Richard*, whilst at anchor in the British Channel, on the night of the 4th October, 1844, the *Richard* being without a light,

In it the Court alluded to the absence of any general rule that a ship at anchor should show a light, adding, it is said to be the custom in the British Channel to show one, but this was rather a general, not a universal practice

Sarah.
4 Ca 98

And similar allusion to the absence of any such general obligation was also made in the case of the *Sarah*, in which that vessel was proceeded against on the part of the *Charles*, for having run foul of her whilst at anchor in the Downs, about two miles from the Gull Light, the *Charles* having exhibited no light

2, Exhibiting Lights

IT HAS BEFORE BEEN STATED, that, although there might exist no general obligation to carry lights, the circumstances of a particular case, such as a peculiar darkness of the night, extreme thickness of the weather, the crowded state of the locality over which the vessel was passing where the collision took place, &c, &c, might point out the exhibition of them as the best if not only means of guarding against accident In such a case, the neglect of the obvious means of prevention might amount to such a culpable neglect of those ordinary measures of prudence, of which every man is bound to make use in the care and employment of his own property, as to deprive a complainant of all legal remedy for any injury which might be reasonably supposed attributable in any considerable degree to such neglect.

The same observations may be applied to the necessity of exhibiting a light upon the occasion of any sudden accidental emergency.

These remarks will be illustrated by the following cases.

In the case of the *Osmanli*, the collision took place between that vessel, a steamer, and the *Cape Packet*, off Cork, at 11 30 P.M. of the 21st December, 1849 7 Ca. 507.

It did not appear from the evidence that it was a very dark night, or very peculiar weather The steamer was running under both sail and steam, about six knots an hour, but there was some doubt whether the *Cape Packet* had exhibited a light *three* or *eight* minutes before the collision

On the part of the *Osmanli*, it was contended that the accident was to be attributed to the schooner not having exhibited a light in due time.

The Court again observed, that it had been determined that there is no general obligation to carry a light, at the same time there have been occasions on which, for the sake of avoiding a misfortune, which was in all human probability likely to occur, it became the duty of a vessel to show one; thus, in the case of the *Fairy*, it was determined that in the river *Mersey*, on a very dark night, a vessel, being towed up to St. George's Dock, should have shown a light, but this was an exception to a general rule.

7 Ca. 509
Fairy.

The Trinity Masters, taking into consideration the speed at which the *Osmanli* was proceeding, about six knots an hour, were of opinion that even three minutes, the shorter of the two times, were sufficient to enable her to wear, and the Court condemned her in the damages.

5 M L M 46.
Oratava

The *Oratava* was a case of collision between that vessel, a Spanish brigantine, and the British brig *Janet*, which took place off Dungeness, about 11 P.M. Dec. 9, 1838.

It appeared in evidence that the night was dark and hazy, and that no light was seen on board the *Janet*.

Vide note, p 4.

The Trinity Masters expressed their opinion that the *Janet* should have had a light, or one ready to exhibit, in order to show her situation and course; but as the other vessel was also to blame, the Court decreed the damage to be divided.

1 Ca. 592
Athol.

The *Athol* was a case of collision between that vessel, in H.M Service, and the *Jane Clark*, which occurred on the 7th March, 1840, off the Lizard. It appeared in evidence that the vessels were coming end on, H.M Ship with the wind free, the *Jane Clark* on a wind, that the night was dark and cloudy, and that no light was shown on board the latter vessel.

The Court, in addressing the Trinity Masters, observed, "I shall have to ask you whether, in your opinion, the absence of any light being shown on board the *Jane Clark*, was such a dereliction of duty, under the circumstances, and taking into consideration the place where she was found, as would impute to her fairly any blame?"

The Trinity Masters expressed their opinion that no blame was attributable to her.

Again, the case of the *Benares* was one of collision which occurred between that vessel and the barque the *Royal Archer*, at sea, in lat. 6° 7′ N., and long 19° 42′ 30″ W

7 Ca 538

Benares

On the part of the *Benares*, the accident was attributed to the neglect of the *Royal Archer* in not having shown a light.

The Court, addressing the Trinity Masters, observed, You will recollect with regard to showing lights, that generally speaking, in the open sea, there is no general obligation to show a light, though under peculiar circumstances it may be obligatory; but generally speaking, in the open sea, it is not incumbent upon a merchant vessel to show a light

The *Stadacona* was a case of collision between that vessel, an Austrian brig, and the *Isabella*, which took place about 2 A.M of March 31, 1847, off the Lizard.

5 Ca. 372

Stadacona.

The *Stadacona* was coming down the Channel on the larboard tack, the *Isabella* was on the starboard tack, and as soon as she discovered the brig she showed a light ahead and kept her course The Court, in requesting the opinion of the Trinity Masters, whether the *Isabella* was free from blame, observed, that she certainly did right in showing a light. The Trinity Masters attributed the blame to the *Stadacona*, and the Court condemned her in the damages.

In the case of the *Columbine*, the owners of the *Undaunted*, a brig, proceeded against that vessel, a steamer, to recover damages for injury sustained, in consequence of a collision which took place between them in the Swin, about 1 A M of the 3rd October, 1842

There was much contradiction in the evidence respecting the state of the night. It appeared that the *Undaunted* was first seen by the other vessel, distant three or four vessels' length.

One of the grounds of defence urged on behalf of the *Columbine* was, that the *Undaunted* was to blame for not having hoisted a light as soon as she perceived that vessel

The Court, observing upon the discrepancy in the evidence, expressed its opinion, that with reference to the state of the night the result appeared to be, that it was such as described by the master of the *Columbine*, viz., that it was dark and somewhat hazy; adding, that if a good look-out had been kept on board the *Columbine*, it would be difficult to say that she ought not to have seen the *Undaunted* at a greater distance than three or four ships' length, and with respect to the obligation of hoisting a light, observed, that there was a broad distinction between constantly carrying a light and hoisting one, but that whether it was incumbent on the *Undaunted* to hoist a light, under the circumstances, was a question for the judgment of the Trinity Masters

In reply to this appeal, the Trinity Masters expressed an opinion that the blame was solely attributable to the *Columbine*, and thus thereby impliedly absolved the *Undaunted* from being in fault in not hoisting a light.

In the case of the *Iron Duke*, before cited,[1] a similar

Iron Duke.

defence was raised, that if it was not the duty of the vessel with which the collision took place, to carry a light, yet it was her duty to have exhibited one, that was to say, she ought to have been prepared with a light, and to have exhibited it upon descrying the steamer.

This was, in a similar manner, left to the judgment of the Trinity Masters, but they denied the existence of any such obligation.

In the case of the *Londonderry*, also before cited,[1] one ground on which the defence was rested, was, that the vessel proceeding against her had not hoisted a light, nor indeed had the means of doing so, at the time of the collision.

After some consideration the Court, though with much reluctance, declared that it was not incumbent on sailing vessels to hoist lights, merely for the purpose of having their particular position noticed by other vessels, and that according to the general principle, as settled in the cases of the *Rose* and *Iron Duke*, there was no obligation on a sailing vessel to hoist lights except when she was in want of a pilot, but that in not hoisting a light there may be shown, under the circumstances of particular cases, such evidence of gross folly or wilful neglect as to disentitle a complainant to any relief.

Where, however, a light has been exhibited, the question often arises, whether this has been done in sufficient time.

Thus, in the case of the *Osmanli*, before cited,[2] and where the particulars of the case are detailed, the Trinity Masters were of opinion that a period of three minutes was sufficient to enable a steamer, going at the rate of six knots an hour, to wear, and to render her responsible for the damage.

The *Clyde* was a case of collision, in which the Danish

Clyde

[1] P 4   [2] P 7

2 Sp 30
Oct. 20,
1854.

schooner *Catharina Ferdinando* proceeded against that vessel, a steamer, on account of a collision, which took place between them about six miles off Flamborough Head, about 2 A M of the 6th December, 1853

It appeared in evidence that the light of the steamer was seen a very considerable time antecedent to the collision, and on her part it was contended that the collision was mainly attributable to the delay on the part of the schooner in showing a light.

On the part of the schooner, it was alleged that, although the weather was dark, vessels could be seen at a considerable distance, that when the master of the vessel first saw the light of the steamer, he was in doubt whether it was on shore or not, and did nothing until the time when it was ascertained to be a steamer, the lantern was then shown over the starboard side, on which quarter the light of the steamer appeared

In reply to a question put by the Court to the Trinity Masters, whether there was any improper delay in showing a light to the steamer, and whether that delay was a contributing cause to the collision, they stated that there was delay, but that it was exhibited as soon as it was known that the light previously seen was that of a steamer. The Court pronounced for the schooner against the *Clyde*.

SUCH ARE THE PRINCIPLES applicable to the question of "lights," as founded upon the general custom and usage of the sea, and which were adopted by almost all countries. These during the earlier stages of commerce, and up to a comparatively recent period, were found sufficient to insure safety in navigating the high seas; within the last few years, however, and more particularly since the use of steam vessels has become so general, the change which has taken place in commercial transactions, and everything connected with them, has been so extraordinary and beyond all calculation, as imperatively to demand the interference of Legislation Not only has the number of the vessels employed multiplied to such an extent as, under certain circumstances, to be a cause of danger, but the size of many vessels is of such magnitude, and the rapidity of their motion so great compared with the movement of former times, as to completely change the character of the accidents to which they may be exposed

In those of former days, although the injury might be considerable, the extent of it was much diminished by the anticipation of the collision, and the consequent provision made against it which were in many cases possible. A collision now is more generally sudden in its occurrence, and between vessels of considerable bulk, acted upon by moving powers of great intensity, and the result too frequently a destruction of property fearful to contemplate, accompanied in some cases with the more serious loss of many of the crew, and one of the vessels themselves

As the first commercial power, and one in whose service the use of steam-vessels on the open ocean had been introduced, Great Britain was also the first to feel the want and necessity of legislative enactment, and in the year 1846 an Act was introduced into Parliament, for the purpose of empowering the Lords of the Admiralty to make such regulations as they should deem desirable respecting the exhibition of lights.

This Act, 9 & 10 Vict, c. 100 received the Royal Assent the 28th August, 1846, and came into operation on the 1st January, 1847.

Legislative enactments, 9 & 10 V, c. 100

In connection with this Act, a series of experiments was

conducted under the direction of the Lords of the Admiralty, for the purpose of testing the power of different kinds of lights.

The result of these experiments proved that, the colour being imparted to them by a lens, a green light might be distinctly seen at the distance of three, and a red one at the distance of two miles, in the ordinary state of the atmosphere at night, a distance amply sufficient to afford time for determining the manner in which the vessel was steering, and adopting the steps necessary to avoid a collision.

A committee was also appointed, composed of officers of the Royal Navy and members of the Mercantile Service, who, from their experience as nautical men, were well qualified to examine and pronounce an opinion upon such a subject; they proceeded to examine as witnesses such persons as were considered best able to supply them with information, and made their Report to their Lordships.

Founded upon this Report, and by virtue of the authority conferred upon them by the Act of Parliament just cited, the Lords of the Admiralty laid down, and duly published, certain regulations, dated 29th June, 1848, enjoining the exhibition of lights by steam-vessels.

These regulations were officially communicated to the other Powers of Europe, with the expression of a hope that upon examination they might consider them applicable to their own subjects, and might be induced to adopt similar ones for the use of vessels sailing under their flag, and thus establish one universal code of navigation in this respect. This wish has been generally very favourably responded to.

As, however, it had been principally with respect to steam-vessels that the want of positive regulations had been felt, to them the provisions of the Act were limited, the benefit, however, which, it was soon felt, had attended the introduction of these regulations, induced the English Government soon afterwards to pass a second Act empowering the Lords of the Admiralty to establish, alter, and revoke from time to time regulations respecting the exhibition of "lights" by all classes of vessels. This Act, 14 & 15 Vict, c. 79, which received the Royal Assent on the 7th August, 1851, came into operation on the 31st December of the same year. [14 & 15 V c. 79]

The subject of the exhibition of "lights" by sea-going vessels was again referred by their Lordships to a well-selected committee; they were divided in opinion respecting the use of the same description of coloured lights by steam and sailing vessels, and, having drawn up a full and able Report on the matters submitted to them, ultimately determined to retain the coloured light for steamers, and require other vessels to show a bright light when there appeared any probability of a collision between them and another vessel, and all classes of vessels to exhibit a light when at anchor.

Upon this Report, correspondent regulations were formed: these came into operation on the 1st August, 1852 and by them the preceding ones were revoked. Similar regulations were also adopted in the Royal Navy, under an Order dated June 12, 1852.

In the year 1854, the Merchant Shipping Act was introduced into Parliament, for the purpose of consolidating and embodying, in one Act, the different enactments relating to maritime matters, scattered over the Statute Book, and of forming one system of legislation applicable to the Mercantile Navy, and with reference to this subject, the clauses [Merchant Shipping Act, 1854, 17 & 18 V, c. 104.]

No 296, 298, 299, were introduced, similar in character to those contained in the former Acts.

This Act, 17 & 18 Vict, c 104, received the Royal Assent 10th August, 1854, and came into operation 1st May, 1855

No new regulations have as yet been made under the authority of the last Act, and as will be more fully explained those of 1852 have been held to be still in force

For the facility of comparison, the clauses of these different Acts of Parliament, and the respective regulations, are here printed in parallel columns

I.	II.	III
9 & 10 V, c. 100.	14 & 15 V, c 79	*Merchant Shipping Act,* 1854, 17 & 18 V, c. 104
	§ 25. And with respect to the lights to be carried, and other provision to be made for guarding against accidents from collision, be it enacted as follows —	§ coxcv The following Rules shall be observed with regard to lights —
§ 10 And be it enacted,		
That the Lord High Admiral, or the Commissioners for executing the office of Lord High Admiral, may from time to time make Regulations requiring the exhibition of such lights by steam vessels, in such manner, within such places, except the River *Thames* above *Yantlett Creek,* and under such circumstances, as the said Lord High Admiral or the said Commissioners may think fit, and may from	26 The Lord High Admiral, or the Commissioners for executing the office of Lord High Admiral, shall from time to time make Regulations requiring the exhibition of such lights by such classes of vessels, whether steam or sailing vessels, within such places, and under such circumstances, as they think	(1) The Admiralty shall from time to time make Regulations requiring the exhibition of such lights, by such classes of ships, whether steam or sailing ships, within such places, and under such circumstances, as they think

I	II.	III.
9 & 10 V., c 100	14 & 15 V., c. 79.	17 & 18 V., c. 104.
time to time make any other Regulations revoking or altering any previous Regulations.	fit, and may from time to time revoke, alter, or vary the same, and they	fit, and may from time to revoke, alter, or vary the same
§ 11. And be it enacted, That the said Lord High Admiral or the said Commissioners shall cause such Regulations, as soon as conveniently may be after the same shall have been made, to be published in four successive *London Gazettes*, and the same shall be deemed to be in force from the date of the last of such publications until the same shall have been altered or revoked, and such alteration or revocation shall have been twice published in like manner as aforesaid.	shall cause such Regulations to be published in the *London Gazette* and to be otherwise publicly made known, and such Regulations shall come into operation on a day to be named in such *Gazette*, and they shall cause such Regulations to be printed, and shall furnish a copy thereof to any Owner or Master of a vessel who applies for the same, and production of the *Gazette* containing such Regulations shall be sufficient evidence of the purport and due making thereof, and	(3) All Regulations made in pursuance of this section shall be published in the *London Gazette*, and shall come into operation on a day to be named in the *Gazette* in which they are published, and the Admiralty shall cause all such Regulations to be printed, and shall furnish a copy thereof to any Owner or Master of a ship who applies for the same, and production of the *Gazette* containing such Regulations shall be sufficient evidence of the due making and purport thereof
§ 12 And be it enacted, That the Master or other person having the charge of any steam vessel which shall be in any river or narrow channel in *Great Britain* or *Ireland*, or the adjacent islands, or upon the sea within twenty miles of any part of the coast of *Great Britain* or *Ireland* shall, whether under weigh or at anchor, be-	all Owners and Masters, or persons having charge of vessels, shall be bound to take notice of the same, and shall, so long as the same continue in force, exhibit	(4) All Owners and Masters shall be bound to take notice of the same, and shall, so long as the same continue in force, exhibit such

I 9 & 10 V., c. 100	II 14 & 15 V., c. 79	III. 17 & 18 V., c. 104
tween sunset and sunrise, exhibit such lights within such places, in such manner, and under such circumstances, as by the said Regulations hereinbefore authorized to be made by the said Lord High Admiral or by the said Commissioners shall be required, and in default thereof shall forfeit and pay a sum not exceeding twenty pounds for every night in which such default shall be made.	such lights, and no others, at such times, within such places, in such manner, and under such circumstances, as are enjoined by such Regulations, and in case of default, the Master or other person having charge of any vessel, or the Owner of such vessel, if it appears that he was in fault, shall, for each and every occasion upon which such Regulations are infringed, forfeit and pay a sum not exceeding twenty pounds. Provided always, That all Regulations made by the said Lord High Admiral, or Commissioners for executing the office of Lord High Admiral, under the authority of the said recited Acts or either of them, and in force at the passing of this Act, together with the penalties applicable thereto, shall continue and be in force as if the same had been made under this Act, until the same be revoked.	lights, at such times, within such places, in such manner, and under such circumstances, as are enjoined by such Regulations, and shall not exhibit any other lights, and in case of default, the Master or the Owner of the ship, if it appears that he was in fault, shall for each occasion upon which such Regulations are infringed, incur a penalty not exceeding twenty pounds.
	§ 28. If in any case of a collision between two or more vessels it appear that such collision was occasioned by the non	§ ccxcviii. If in any case of collision it appears to the court, before which the case is tried, that such collision

I.	II.	III
9 & 10 *V.*, c. 100	14 & 15 *V.*, c. 79.	17 & 18 *V.*, c. 104.
	observance either of the foregoing Rules with respect to the passing of steamers, or of the Rules to be made as aforesaid by the Lord High Admiral, or the Commissioners for executing the office of Lord High Admiral, with respect to the exhibition of lights, the Owner of the vessel by which any such Rule has been infringed shall not be entitled to recover any recompense whatsoever for any damage sustained by such vessel in such collision unless it appears to the court before which the case is tried that the circumstances of the case were such as to justify a departure from the Rule, and in case any damage to person or property be sustained in consequence of the non-observance of any of the said Rules, the same shall in all courts of justice be deemed, in the absence of proof to the contrary, to have been occasioned by the wilful default of the Master or other person having the charge of such vessel, and such Master or other person shall, unless it appears to the court	was occasioned by the non-observance of any Rule for the exhibition of lights, issued in pursuance of the powers hereinbefore contained,
And the Owner of any steam vessel in which such light shall not be exhibited as aforesaid, shall not be entitled to recover any recompense or damage whatsoever which may be sustained by such vessel in consequence of any other vessel running foul thereof during the night.		the Owner of the ship by which such Rule has been infringed shall not be entitled to recover any recompence whatever for any damage sustained by such ship in such collision, unless it is shown to the satisfaction of the court that the circumstances of the case made a departure from the Rule necessary
§ 13. And be it enacted, That if any damage to any person or property shall be sustained in consequence of the non-observance as respects any steam vessels of the Rules contained in the two Enactments relative to the passing of steam vessels, and to the exhibiting of lights hereinbefore contained, the same shall in all courts of justice be deemed, in the absence of proof to the contrary, to have		§ ccxcix In case any damage to person or property arises from the non-observance by any ship of any of the said Rules, such damage shall be deemed to have been occasioned by the wilful default of the person in charge of the deck of of such ship at the time, unless it is shown to the satisfaction of the court that the circumstances

I.	II.	III.
9 & 10 *V.*, c. 100	14 & 15 *V*, c 79	17 & 18 *V.*, c. 104.
been occasioned by the wilful default of the Master or other person having the charge of such steam vessel, and such master or other person shall be subject in all proceedings, whether civil or criminal, to the legal consequences of such wilful default.	before which the case is tried that the circumstances of the case were such as to justify a departure from the Rule, be subject in all proceedings, whether civil or criminal, to the legal consequences of such default.	of the case made a departure from the Rule necessary

17 & 18 V., c. 120.

By a subsequent Act, "The Merchant Shipping Repeal "Act, 1854," certain Acts, and amongst them the 14 & 15 Vict, c. 79, were repealed, with the provision

" That such appeal should not affect
" Any appointment, bye-law, regulation, or license, duly
  " made or granted under any enactment thereby re-
  " pealed, and subsisting at the time when that Act
  " came into operation; and the same should continue
  " in force, but should be subject to such provisions of
  " the Merchant Shipping Act, 1854, as were applicable thereto respectively."

REGULATIONS AS TO LIGHTS.

I.

REGULATIONS *under* 9 & 10 V., c. 100.
1848
Since Revoked.
STEAMERS' LIGHTS TO PREVENT COLLISION.

By the Commissioners for executing the office of Lord High Admiral of the United Kingdom of Great Britain and Ireland, &c., &c.

Whereas, in consequence of the increase which has taken place in the number of steam vessels, and the want of an adequate and uniform system of night lights, a great number of accidents have arisen from vessels running foul of each other at night, involving not only the destruction of valuable property to a considerable amount, but also a great loss of human life, and whereas We have been empowered by Act of Parliament passed in the tenth year of Her present Majesty, entitled an "Act for the Regulation of Steam Navigation," to make such Regulations as we may deem proper for the exhibition of lights by steam vessels, with the view of obviating a recurrence of the disasters above referred to We do, therefore, in virtue of the power and authority vested in us by the said Act hereby require and direct that all British steam vessels (whether propelled by paddles or screws), including those belonging to Her Majesty, shall

9 & 10 Vict., c. 100.

II.

REGULATIONS *under* 14 & 15 V., c. 79.
1852.

ADMIRALTY NOTICE RESPECTING LIGHTS TO BE CARRIED BY SEA-GOING VESSELS TO PREVENT COLLISION.

By the Commissioners for executing the office of Lord High Admiral of the United Kingdom of Great Britain and Ireland, &c., &c.

By virtue of the power and authority vested in us by the Act 14 and 15 Victoria, c. 79, dated 7th August, 1851. We hereby require and direct that the following Regulations be strictly observed

STEAM VESSELS

All British sea-going steam vessels (whether propelled by paddles or screws) shall, within all seas, gulfs, channels, straits, bays, creeks, roads, roadsteads, harbours, havens, ports, and rivers, and under all circum-

not in 1858.

I.
REGULATIONS of 1848
Since Revoked

between sunset and sunrise exhibit lights of such description, and in such manner, as is hereinafter mentioned viz.,

When under Steam or Sail

A Bright White Light at the foremast head
A Green Light on the starboard side.
A Red Light on the port side

When at Anchor: A Common Bright Light

Having reference to the foregoing, the following Rules are to be observed viz.,

1 The Masthead light is to be visible at the distance of at least five miles in the dark with a clear atmosphere, and the Lantern is to be so constructed as to show a uniform and unbroken light over an arc of the horizon of twenty points of the compass, being ten points on each side of the ship viz., from right ahead to two points abaft the beam on either side

2 The green light on the starboard side is to be visible at the distance of at least two miles in a dark night with a clear atmosphere, and the lantern is to be so constructed as to show a uniform and unbroken light over an arc of the horizon of ten points of the compass viz., from right ahead to two points abaft the beam on the starboard side The lantern on the port side is likewise to be fitted so as to throw its red light the same distance, and over a similar arc on that side.

3 The side lights are moreover to

II
REGULATIONS of 1852.

stances, between sunset and sunrise, exhibit lights of such description, and in such manner, as hereinafter mentioned viz.,

When under Steam.

A Bright White Light at the foremast head
A Green Light on the starboard side.
A Red Light on the port side

1. The Masthead light is to be visible at a distance of *at least five miles* in a dark night with a clear atmosphere, and the Lantern is to be so constructed as to show a uniform and unbroken light over an arc of the horizon of twenty points of the compass, being ten points on each side of the ship· viz., from right ahead to two points abaft the beam on either side

2. The green light on the starboard side is to be visible at a distance of *at least two miles* in a dark night with a clear atmosphere; and the lantern is to be so constructed as to show a uniform and unbroken light over an arc of the horizon of ten points of the compass viz., from right ahead to two points abaft the beam on the starboard side.

3 The red light on the port side is likewise to be fitted so as to throw its light the same distance on that side

4. The side lights are moreover

I.
REGULATIONS *of* 1848.
Since Revoked.

be fitted with inboard screens of at least three feet long, to prevent the lights from being seen across the bow. The screens are to be placed in a fore and aft line with the inner edge of the side lights

The lantern used when at anchor is to be so constructed as to show a good light all round the horizon

Masters or other persons having the charge of steam vessels are hereby further required to take notice, that in the event of their neglecting to comply with the above Regulations, they shall, under the provisions of the Act before quoted, "forfeit and pay a sum not exceeding Twenty Pounds *for every night* in which such default shall be made, and the Owner of any steam vessel in which such light shall not be exhi

II.
REGULATIONS *of* 1852.

to be fitted with screens on the inboard side of at least three feet long, to prevent the lights from being seen across the bow

When at Anchor A Common Bright Light.

SAILING VESSELS

We hereby require that all sailing vessels, when under sail, or being towed, approaching or being approached by any other vessel, shall be bound to show between sunset and sunrise a bright light, in such a position as can be best seen by such vessel or vessels, and in sufficient time to avoid collision

All sailing vessels *at anchor* in roadsteads or fairways shall be also bound to exhibit between sunset and sunrise a constant <u>bright light at the masthead</u>, except within harbours or other places where Regulations for other lights for ships are legally established

The lantern to be used when at anchor, both by steam vessels and sailing vessels, is to be so constructed as to show a clear good light all round the horizon.

WE HEREBY revoke all Regulations heretofore made by us relating to steam vessels exhibiting or carrying lights, and we require that the preceding Regulations be strictly carried into effect on and after the 1st of August, 1852

I.
Regulations of 1848
Since Revoked.

bited as aforesaid, shall not be entitled to recover any recompense or damage whatsoever which may be sustained by such vessel in consequence of any vessel running foul thereof during the night.

"And that if any damage to any person or property shall be sustained in consequence of the non observance, as respects any steam vessel, of the Rules contained in the two enactments relative to the passing of Steam vessels, and to the exhibiting of Lights hereinbefore contained, the same will in all Courts of Justice be deemed, in the absence of proof to the contrary, to have been occasioned by the wilful default of the Master or other person having the charge of such steam vessel, and such Master or other person will be subject in all proceedings, whether civil or criminal, to the legal consequences of such wilful default."

The River Thames, above Yantlet Creek, is not included in the above Regulations.

Given under our hands the 29th day of May, 1848.

J. W. D. DUNDAS
M. F. F. BERKELEY.

By command of their Lordships,

W. A. B. HAMILTON.

Illustrations of the foregoing systems of steamers' lights, as directed by the Lords Commissioners of the Admiralty.

The following Diagrams are added

II.
Regulations of 1852.

Given under our hands the 1st day of May, 1852.

HYDE PARKER.
P. HORNBY.

By command of their Lordships,

W. A. B. HAMILTON

25

I.	II.
REGULATIONS *of* 1848.	REGULATIONS of 1852.
Since Revoked	
with a view to illustrate the working of the above system; the letter R signifying a red light, and G a green one.	*Diagrams intended to illustrate the working of this mode of fitting lights*

First Situation.

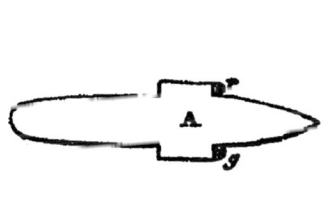 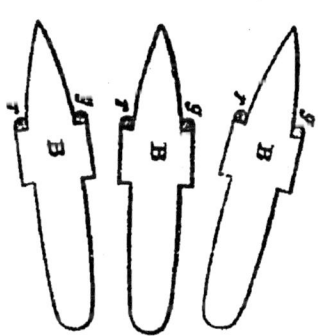

In this situation the steamer A will only see the *red light* of the vessel B in whichsoever of the three positions the latter may happen to be, because the *green light* will be hidden from view, A will be assured that the *port* side of B is towards him, and that the latter is therefore crossing the bows of A in *some direction to port*, A will therefore (if so close as to fear collision) *port* his helm with confidence and pass clear. On the other hand, the vessel B, in either of the three positions, will observe the *red, green,* and *masthead* lights of A in a triangular form, by which the vessel B will know that a steamer is approaching *directly* towards him;—B will act accordingly

It is scarcely necessary to remark that the *masthead* light will always

In this situation, the steamer A will only see the *red light* of the vessel B, in whichsoever of the three positions the latter may happen to be, because the *green* light will be hid from view, A will be assured that the *port* side of B is towards him, and that the latter is therefore crossing the bows of A in *some direction to port*, A will therefore (if so close as to fear collision) *port* his helm with confidence and pass clear. On the other hand, the vessel B, in either of the three positions, will see the *red, green,* and *masthead* lights of A appear in a triangular form, by which the former will know that a steamer is approaching *directly* towards him, B will act accordingly

It is scarcely necessary to remark that the *masthead* light will always

No difference whatever between these two sets of illustrations — except the passages marked — others quite immaterial

26

I.	II.
REGULATIONS *of* 1848. Since Revoked	REGULATIONS *of* 1852
be visible in all directions, *except abaft the beam* of the vessel carrying it	be visible in every situation till abaft the beam.

Second Situation.

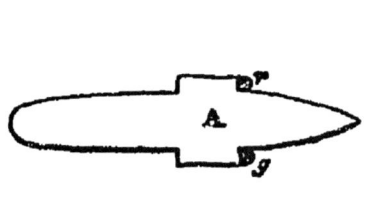 

Here A will see B's *green* light only, which will clearly indicate to A that B is crossing to starboard. Again, A's *three* lights being visible to B, will apprise B that a steamer is steering directly towards him.	Here A will see B's *green* light only, which will clearly indicate to the former that B is crossing to starboard. Again, A's *three* lights being visible to B, will apprise the latter that a steamer is steering directly towards him.

Third Situation.

A and B will see each other's *red* light only, the screens preventing the *green* lights from being seen. Both vessels are evidently passing to *port*.	A and B will see each other's *red* light only, the screens preventing the *green* lights from being seen. Both vessels are evidently passing to *port*.

I. REGULATIONS *of* 1848 Since Revoked.	II. REGULATIONS *of* 1852.

Fourth Situation.

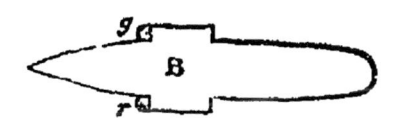

Here a *green* light only will be visible to each vessel, the screens preventing the *red* lights from being seen. The vessels are therefore passing to *starboard*	Here a *green* light only will be visible to each, the screens preventing the *red* lights from being seen. They are therefore passing to *starboard.*

Fifth Situation

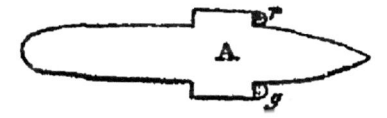

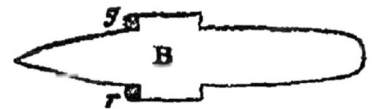

Here the two coloured lights, visible to each vessel, will indicate their *direct* approach towards each other. In this situation, *both should put their helms to* PORT. This Rule is already pretty generally adopted, but it is made *imperative*, and is in all cases to be strictly observed.	Here the two coloured lights, visible to each, will indicate their direct approach towards each other In this situation, both should put their helms to port.
	DIRECTIONS FOR FITTING THE LIGHTS.
The manner of fixing the coloured lights should be particularly attended to; they would require to be fitted each with a *screen* of wood or canvas on the *inboard* side, in order to prevent *both* being seen at the same moment from any direction but that of *right a-head*.	The manner of fixing the coloured lights is to be particularly attended to. They should be fitted, each, with a screen of wood on the inboard side, in order to prevent both being seen at the same moment from any direction but that of right a-head.
This is important, for without the *screens* (a principle first intro-	This is important, for without the *screens* any plan of bow lights

I.
REGULATIONS of 1848
Since Revoked

duced with this system) any plan of bow lights would be ineffective as a means of indicating the *direction in which a steamer may be steering.*

This will be readily understood by a reference to the foregoing illustrations, where it will appear evident that in any situation in which two vessels may approach each other in the dark, the coloured lights will instantly indicate to both the *relative course of each,*—that is, each will know whether the other is approaching *directly,* or *crossing her bows* either to *starboard* or to *port.* This information is all that is required to enable vessels to pass each other freely in the darkest night, with almost equal safety as in broad day, and for the want of which so many lamentable accidents have occurred.

If at anchor, all vessels without distinction are bound to display a common light.

II.
REGULATIONS of 1852.

would be ineffective as a means of indicating the direction of steering.

This will be readily understood by a reference to the preceding illustrations, where it will appear evident that in any situation in which two vessels may approach each other in the dark, the coloured lights will instantly indicate to both the relative course of each,—that is, each will know whether the other is approaching directly, or crossing the bows either to starboard or to port. This intimation is all that is required to enable vessels to pass each other in the darkest night, with almost equal safety as in broad day, and for the want of which so many lamentable accidents have occurred

It is left to all persons concerned to furnish themselves with whatever description of Lantern they may see fit to adopt, provided always that the above conditions are fully and effectually carried out.

By command of their Lordships,

W A B HAMILTON.

Note.—The system of night lights, laid down in the above Regulations, has been adopted in Her Majesty's service, and by the governments of the principal foreign maritime nations.

AN EXAMINATION of the respective clauses in the preceding Acts of Parliament, and the Regulations founded upon them, will show how little they differ from one another; the second Act, that of 14 & 15 Vict., c. 79, being little more than the extension of the former Act, 9 & 10 Vict, c. 100, from steam vessels to all classes of vessels, steam or sailing; and the last Act, the embodying of these clauses in one consolidated Act, that of the Merchant Shipping Act, 1854

The corresponding Regulations are also principally an adaptation of the preceding ones to the altered circumstances arising from the fresh enactments.

IN CONNECTION WITH THESE, the following points demand particular attention:

> The general obligation imposed upon every description of vessel of exhibiting a constant bright light when at anchor
>
> The use of lights between sunset and sunrise by sailing vessels or steamers; the former being required to show a bright light when approaching or being approached by any other vessel, and the latter to make use of coloured fixed lights and screens.
>
> The implied obligation of attention to their being kept in a proper state of burning

And to these may be added, the consideration of the consequences of a non-compliance with the Regulations.

WITH REFERENCE to vessels at anchor, the Regulations require that the lantern to be used is to be so constructed as to show a clear good light all round the horizon,[1] and in the case of sailing vessels this light is to be exhibited at the masthead; an exception to this regulation is made in harbours or other places where other regulations are legally established

Vessels at anchor.

---

[1] V *Adventure,* Jan 8, 1853.

The following are the principal cases which relate to this branch of the subject·

1 Sp 427
May 18,
1854

The case of the *Telegraph* was that of an action brought against that vessel, a steamer, by the barque *Palermo*, on account of a collision which took place between these two vessels about 8 P.M. of the 29th November, 1853, off the coast of Ireland.

The *Palermo* had been brought to anchor in the roadstead, and had a bright signal lantern hoisted in her larboard mizen rigging, which continued to burn there at the time of the collision. The sole question was, whether she had or had not a proper light hoisted.

The Court observed, that the provisions of the Act of Parliament were "that all sailing vessels at anchor in roadsteads or fairways, shall be bound to exhibit between sunset and sunrise a constant bright light at the masthead." The *Palermo* certainly had not complied with this regulation. Upon the whole view of the case, however, the Court, being of opinion that the light as placed was as visible as it would have been at the masthead, decided in favour of the *Palermo*

Against this decision an appeal was made to the Judicial Committee, the judges of which, with reference to the position of the light, observed that, with respect to the expression "at the masthead," they were clearly of opinion it meant at the *very top*; that if the top-gallant mast be standing it must be at the top-gallant mast; whichever is the standing mast that is the mast, for if the lanterns were at the very top it would show a light around the horizon.

Upon other grounds, however, the decision was ultimately reversed

June 23,
1854

The *Argo* was a case of collision between that vessel and the *Bute*, which occurred in the British Channel, between

3 and 4 A.M. on the 28th February, 1854, and in which cross actions were entered by the respective parties

The *Bute* was proceeding from Penarth Roads to Bristol; the *Argo*, on her voyage from Falmouth to Gloucester, had anchored in the Bristol Channel near the light-vessel, and had exhibited, as it was alleged on her behalf, two lights.

The Court, addressing the Trinity Masters, observed that, as in this case the *Argo* was lying at anchor in a roadstead and was therefore, in compliance with the Admiralty Regulations, bound to put up a light, it lay upon her to prove that she had done so, and when this had been done it was then for the other party to show that the light had gone out at the time of the collision. On the part of the *Argo*, it was sworn that she had exhibited two lights, and that they were burning at the time of the collision. On the other hand, it had been sworn, on the part of those on board the *Bute*, that they did not see them. The evidence was nearly balanced; it was for them, therefore, to consider whether it was not best to trust to the affirmative testimony,[1] and this might be done without imputing perjury to the other parties, as, although the light might have been there, they might not have seen it.

The Trinity Masters expressed their opinion that the light was hoisted on board of the *Argo*, and that the collision was solely attributable to the want of a good look-out on board the *Bute*

The Court pronounced for the *Argo* in both actions.

The *Harriett* was a case in which the *William*, a brig, proceeded against that vessel on account of a collision which occurred between them in Yarmouth Roads, about 4 A.M. on the 15th March, 1853

March 2, 1855.

[1] V *Adventure*, Jan 8, 1853

Both vessels had been at anchor; the *Harriett* had just got under weigh, the *William* remaining at anchor, but without a light, as the night was so clear as to induce those on board to consider it unnecessary to hoist one

The Court, without hearing counsel for the defence, expressed its unanimous opinion that the action could not be maintained; and observed that the Act of Parliament was a binding law upon all vessels lying at anchor in a roadstead to hoist a light, and there was no exception whatever to be found in it; nor could the Court engraft any exception upon the rule, because it happened to be a light night, or one in which ships could easily be descried

The presumption of law and the presumption of fact is, that all vessels at anchor have a light hoisted at night in a roadstead, and consequently that all vessels which have no light so hoisted are under weigh; the *Harriett*, therefore, was without doubt justified in assuming the *William* to be a vessel not lying at anchor, but under weigh; and concurred in the opinion of counsel, that the construction to be put upon the Act of Parliament was, that unless the collision was occasioned by the absence of light, and supposing the *Harriett* to be to blame, it would be a case for division of damages. As, however, the case stood, the Court expressed its opinion that the *Harriett* was free from blame, that the *William* was wholly in fault, and dismissed the cause.

April 18, 1856.

In the case of the *Vivid*, the collision took place between that vessel, a steamer, and the brigantine *Henry*, on the 11th August, 1855; the *Henry* having brought up opposite to Dover Harbour.

It appeared in evidence that the *Henry* whilst so at anchor had hung up a signal lantern on a spar under the boom of the foresail

In reply to an assertion made on the part of the *Vivid* that there might have been a light, but that it was not burning at the time in question, the Court, addressing the Trinity Masters, observed, you have the direct evidence of three witnesses that it was burning; it was also in evidence that the light was properly trimmed; and therefore in ordinary presumption and in presumption of law the probability was, that if nothing particular occurred to the contrary, the light continued to burn.

The Trinity Masters having expressed their opinion that a proper light had been hoisted and was burning, upon that and other grounds the Court pronounced in favour of the *Henry*

The *Napoleon III.* was a case of collision, in which the *Good Intent*, a fishing smack, sought to recover damages for a total loss. The collision occurred at 6 P.M of the 17th December, 1855, about fourteen miles from the Start Point

April 26, 1856 Fishing smack

The *Good Intent* was lying with her trawl down, and on descrying the other vessel, lighted a flare up, which after having been for a short time held under the bulwarks was kept burning.

The *Napoleon III* admitted having seen the light at the distance of about a mile and a half, but alleged that it disappeared, and that the collision was occasioned by their having been misled by such disappearance.

The Court, addressing the Trinity Masters, observed that in the first instance it must be remembered that the vessel proceeding against the other was a fishing vessel, lying on her own fishing ground with her trawl attached, so that it was incompetent to her to adopt any measure for her own safety She had been assimilated to a vessel at anchor, and certainly was nearly as incompetent to avoid a collision as if she were lying at anchor ; but it did not follow that she was bound to keep a light up according to the Admiralty Regulations; they applied to a vessel at anchor, and not to one riding on her trawl ; with respect to which, the custom was that it was not usual to keep a light up, but to have one ready to show in case of necessity.

<small>Showing lights</small>

WITH REFERENCE to the use of lights under other circumstances than that of being at anchor, the Regulations require that all sailing vessels, when under sail or being towed, approaching or being approached by any other vessel, shall be bound to show between sunset and sunrise a bright light in such a position as can be best seen by such vessel or vessels, and in sufficient time to avoid collision.

The construction to be put upon this part of the Regulations will be best exemplified by the following cases.

<small>July 2, 1855.</small>

In the case of the *Clyde*, an action was instituted against that vessel by the *George and Eliza*, a schooner, on account of a collision which took place between them, about 9 P.M. on the 19th August, 1854, on the coast of Suffolk.

It appeared in evidence that no light was exhibited by the schooner.

On that point, the Court, in addressing the Trinity Masters, observed, You very well know that the Act of Parliament directs that all vessels shall hoist lights, according to the Regulations prescribed by the Lords of the Admiralty, that sailing vessels, though they are not compelled to carry a light, must have one ready to show, and show it when other vessels appear. There is no limit to that direction at all, except as to the time when it is to be shown —viz, that it must take place after sunset and before sunrise. There is no doubt that the schooner was wrong in not showing a light.

The case of the *Gloria Deo* was one of collision between that vessel, a brig of 152 tons, and the *Anna*, a sloop of 53 tons, which took place on 23rd January, 1854, off Beachy Head.

Oct 29, 1855.

It appeared from the evidence that the *Anna* had a bright signal lantern hung upon the cross-tree, that the night was dark, and that she had descried the other vessel at a distance of about 150 yards; that the *Gloria Deo* had no light, and on her part it was contended that the collision was one of inevitable accident, owing to the blackness of the night, which prevented her seeing the *Anna* until they were close upon her, and unable to avoid it.

The Court observed, that if the *Anna* could discern the *Gloria Deo* at the distance of 150 yards, although carrying no light, that the latter vessel might have discerned the former carrying one, although of so much smaller size, at a greater distance, and ought to have guarded against the collision by timely precaution.

The case of the *Imperatriz* was that of an action brought against that vessel, a steamer, by the brig *John Bunyan*, on account of a collision which occurred between them in the Sea of Marmora, about 10 P.M of the 17th August, 1856

May 12, 1856

The brig was bound from Constantinople to Syra, the steamer was proceeding from Ireland to the Crimea with troops; there was a moderate breeze from east north east

It appeared in evidence that the brig had observed the steamer distant three miles a-head; she ported her helm, the signal lantern was taken from the bowsprit, and exhibited over the port bow The steamer just before the collision had starboarded her helm.

The Court pronounced the opinion of the Trinity Masters to be that the steamer was in fault, and condemned her in the damages

D 2

1 Sp 206
Nov 17,
1853

The *Clarence* was a case of collision between that vessel, a steamer, and the brig *Maria*, which occurred off the coast of Norfolk, between 10 and 11 P.M of 6th March, 1853.

There was much discrepancy in the evidence, particularly upon the point whether the *Maria* had exhibited a light. Four witnesses swore directly to the point, and the master of that vessel gave a particular description of the lantern used on the occasion, that it had eight squares and plate glass round it, that the burner of the lamp was one inch wide, and of a proportionate thickness Objections were taken to this minuteness of description as if prepared for the occasion, but the Court observed that there really was nothing extraordinary in it, because a signal lamp, which is now required by law, but which was not required until within a short period ago, was a matter that would make an impression on the mind of the master He knows what lamp he uses and sees constantly. The Trinity Masters, after the case had been argued, on this and other grounds ultimately expressed an opinion in favour of the *Maria*, implying therefore that she had lights. This sentence was affirmed on appeal, by the Judicial Committee, and an opinion expressed by that Court that the *Maria* had lights.

Jan 29,
1856

In the case of the *Ericson*, that vessel, a steamer, had run down the barque *Alderman Thompson*, off Dover, on the 15th October, 1855, about midnight.

It appeared in evidence that the barque was proceeding from Portsmouth to Sunderland, with a fresh breeze from N W by N on the port tack heading E N E, when she observed the green light of the steamer broad on her starboard bow, distant about four miles, and thereupon exhibited a bright light in a large signal lantern off that bow; that the steamer was proceeding on W S.W. course at the rate of ten knots an hour at the time of the collision.

Some discussion took place as to the kind of light which was exhibited by the *Alderman Thompson*.

The Court, with respect to this, observed that the Trinity Masters had given it as their opinion that it was of the description ordinarily shown, that the barque did all that she ought to have done in showing a light from the starboard bow, and that from that bow it was shown in a proper direction to a steamer approaching with her green light, and pronounced the *Ericson* in fault.

In the case of the *Argo*, the barque *Arthur Wellesley* proceeded against that vessel, a schooner, on account of a collision which occurred between them on the 14th September, 1855.

Jan, 25, 1856

The night, it appeared, was dark, and there was some discrepancy in the evidence with respect to the wind. On the part of the *Arthur Wellesley*, the party proceeding, and in proof that she was free from blame, it was alleged that she was close-hawled on the starboard tack, and that as soon as she descried the other vessel a lighted lantern was held up, and her helm was ported.

On that of the *Argo*, it was contended that the wind was E, and that she was steering S.E by E when she saw the *Arthur Wellesley* at the distance of four hundred yards and ported her helm, but not perceiving that the vessel had altered her course, she starboarded her helm and the collision took place.

The Court, addressing the Trinity Masters, observed, that with respect to the showing of the lantern the master swore to it directly, and so did another witness, who swore that he was the very individual who took the lantern from the companion of the ship, and that there was no reason why their affidavit should not be credited. If then the light was shown as soon as it could be, and the helm put to port as soon as possible, what more could have been done to avoid collision?

The Trinity Masters pronounced the *Argo* to be in fault, and condemned her in the damages.

May 3, 1856

The *Telegraph* was a case of collision between that vessel, a steamer, and the *Robert Burrell*, a brig, which took place off Cromer about 10 P M of the 3rd December, 1855.

The night, it appeared, was dark and cloudy, and on the part of the *Robert Burrell*, it was alleged that, on descrying the other vessel at a distance of about two miles, her helm was ported, and a bright light held over the port bow

On that of the *Telegraph*, it was contended that the collision occurred almost immediately after the light was seen

The Court observed, that if the light was only exhibited when the steamer was within one hundred or two hundred yards, that vessel would not be to blame. The evidence, however, on the part of the schooner was that the steamer was seen at the distance of two miles, when the mate ordered a light to be brought to him, and when he had got it, but before he exhibited it, directed the helm to be ported, adding, that it was a question for the consideration of the Trinity Masters, whether, when a steamer is seen a mile and a half or two miles off, the prudent course is not to show a light, and then port the helm, little time being allowed for discretion The Trinity Masters expressed their opinion that the *Robert Burrell* was not in fault, that a bad look-out was kept on board the *Telegraph*, and the Court condemned her in the damages

WITH RESPECT TO STEAMERS, the Regulations require them to exhibit three coloured fixed lights·

    A bright white light at the foremast head,

    A green light on the starboard side,

    A red light on the port side,

and that these lights should be of a certain power. They also require the side lights to be fitted with certain screens, so as to prevent the lights from being seen across the bow.

The former Regulations required their use by steamers when under steam or sail, the latter, when under steam.

Upon this subject, and also with reference to the necessity of a proper attention to the burning of the lamp, the following cases may be referred to·

In the case of the *Rob Roy*, which was a case of collision between that steamer and another steamer, the *Unicorn*, it appeared in evidence that the green light of the *Unicorn* had, just before the collision, been accidentally extinguished, and the other vessel had in consequence been deceived in its opinion of the course to be pursued by her. Had that light been visible, she would have known it to have been a steamer, and have been bound to obey the Admiralty Regulations, and have starboarded her helm; but in consequence of it not appearing, and only a bright light being visible, she considered the vessel to be coming end on, and adopted the recognised rule of navigation and put her helm to port.

The Court, assisted by the Trinity Masters, was of opinion that she was perfectly justified in the course she adopted, and dismissed the action, observing upon the necessity and utmost importance that those on board the steamer should see that the three lights are duly lighted and kept burning

margin: Steamers

margin: 3 W.R. 191. Nov. 28, 1849

The case of the *Swanland* was that of an action brought against that vessel, a steamer, by another steamer, the *Jupiter*, on account of a collision which took place in the Humber, about 3 A M of the 17th August, 1854, one vessel being in the act of quitting the port of Hull, the other of entering it

The question depended upon the fact what lights were carried by the *Jupiter*

Upon this point the Court observed that two things were necessary. 1st, that the lamps should be of the capacity required by the statute, by which was meant capability and power, and 2ndly, that they should be burning brightly at the time. And that the burden of proof was upon the *Jupiter*, 1st, because those on board that vessel allege the affirmative; and 2ndly, because the state of the lamps, their original condition and construction, and their state at the time of the collision, are matters peculiarly within the knowledge of those on board And it is a maxim or rule of law, which may be and has been in well-known cases carried to the greatest extreme, that the burden of proof should under all circumstances be thrown on those who have a peculiar knowledge of the subject, and peculiar means of proving it, which do not belong to the other party; and proceeded to point out the difference between proceedings in the Common-Law Courts and the Admiralty Court, that in the former the plaintiff must be entirely free from blame, but that in the Admiralty Court the vessel proceeding against the other might recover part of the damage, as the rule was, where both parties are wrong, to divide the whole damage done to both vessels, each paying half

The Court, assisted by the Trinity Masters, was of opinion that the lamps were of the proper construction and power, but that it was not satisfactorily proved that they were burning brightly and properly at the time of collision, though it did not think that any deficiency of the lamps occasioned it. Under all the circumstances, it was held that both parties were to blame, and that the damage must be divided.[1]

The *Sylph* was a case of collision between that vessel and the steamer the *Meteor*, which occurred in the River on the evening of the 18th December, 1853.

2 Sp 75, 85 Dec. 14, 1854

On the part of the *Meteor*, it was pleaded that on leaving Blackwall a lantern was suspended in front of the funnel, and another attached to the bowsprit. Both lanterns were supplied with large masthead candles, which had been lighted and were burning brightly when she left Blackwall, but that just before the collision the flame of the candle in the lantern at the bowsprit accidentally and unaccountably went out, and having been re-lighted while the snuff still retained a dead light, was in the act of being replaced when the collision took place.

The Court observed, with respect to the lights, that it appeared from the evidence that the steamer had two lights originally when going down the River, but that one of the lights, that at the bowsprit, had gone out. And it is a question for your decision whether that was, in your opinion, a sufficient reason for those on board the *Sylph* to believe the *Meteor* to be a vessel at anchor and not in motion. And a most important question it is; because, though the *Meteor* may not be in any degree to blame for the light going out, for lights will go out at sea as well as elsewhere, it might be an accident, yet it is the same, as regards the other party, as if it had arisen from negligence; she must suffer the consequence of the light going out if she misled the *Sylph*

[1] V p 32

The Trinity Masters were of opinion that the *Sylph* was misled by the bowsprit light of the *Meteor* having gone out, in consequence of which she was mistaken for a vessel at anchor; but that as the *Sylph* herself was in other respects to blame, the Court pronounced both parties to be in fault, and decreed the damage to be divided

AS AN ADDITIONAL MEANS of enforcing the observance of these Regulations, it is enacted by the 14 & 15 Vict, c 79, § 28, and 17 & 18 Vict., c. 104, § 298, that in case a collision should be occasioned by the non-observance of this Rule, the owners of the vessel infringing the Rule shall not be entitled to recover damages for the injury sustained by it.

V p 18.

This enactment has been frequently brought before the Court. The following decisions are those in which it has been held that the want of observance of the Rule has not occasioned the collision,[1] and that the owners therefore have not been precluded from recovering compensation.

Neglect of rule not occasion of collision.

The *Panther* was the case of an action brought against that vessel by the schooner *New Union*, on account of a collision between these two vessels about six o'clock A.M. of the 18th December, 1852, off the Nore Light;

1 Sp 35 May 25, 1853

In the discussion of which much stress was laid upon the Regulations of the Admiralty

It was an admitted fact that the *New Union* did not show a light when she saw the steamer, and the Court observed, that it was abundantly clear that the Rule to do so was binding upon her, but, as by the 28th section of the 14 & 15 Vict., c 79 (which was then in force), it was enacted, that if the collision was occasioned by the non-observance of the Rule, the owners of such vessel so neglecting it shall not be entitled to compensation The

V. p 18

[1] V *Adventure*, Jan. 8 1853

question, in that respect, resolved itself into this: whether the collision was occasioned in whole or in part by the schooner omitting to show a light.

The answer given by the Trinity Masters to this question was, certainly not, for according to the statement of the steamer herself, she saw the schooner in ample time to have avoided the collision.

The Court, being satisfied by the evidence on other points, pronounced in favour of the schooner, condemning the *Panther* in the damages.

The case of the *Boreas* was one of collision between that vessel and the *Adam Clarke*, which occurred about 11 45 P.M on the 9th May, 1853, off Flamborough Head, and in which cross actions were brought against each other by the owners of the different vessels.[1]

Feb 3, 1854.

It appeared, in evidence, the *Boreas* was descried by the other vessel at the distance of a quarter of a mile, and that neither of them showed a light.

Upon this latter point, the Court observed, that it did not appear that this collision was occasioned by the want of showing a light at all, for according to the statement of

---

[1] "It is customary" in the Court of Admiralty, where there is any doubt as to the party to whom the blame attaches, for each to bring their action against the other an arrangement is then made by the respective Proctors that the decision in one case shall govern that in the other; this is entered as a minute by the Registrar in the Assignation Book, and by this means the expenses of two actions are almost reduced to those of one. This is a practice highly approved of by the Court, it is not obligatory,[2] but unless some good reason were shown for a deviation from it, the Court would mark its disapprobation in any question of costs which might come before it in the course of the suit

Cross actions.

---

[1] *Calypso*, January 13, 1856
[2] *Seringapatam*, 6 Cu 171, *Calypso*, January 13, 1856

both parties they saw each other in ample time to have avoided a collision, provided proper measures had been adopted for that purpose.

<small>Feb 5, 1854</small>

The case of the *Louise* was one of collision between that vessel and the brig *Elswick*, which occurred off Whitby about 10 30 P M of the 15th October, 1853

It appeared in evidence that neither vessel showed a light, and on behalf of the *Louise* the accident was attributed to this neglect on the part of the other vessel.

Upon which the Court observed, that such an objection came with a very indifferent grace from a vessel that never attempted to show a light and had not one ready to show, although she had one ready to be lighted; and as the Trinity Masters expressed their opinion that the *Elswick* had not caused the collision by not exhibiting a light, but that the cause of it was the want of a good look-out on board the *Louise*, the Court pronounced against that vessel.

<small>1 Sp 217 Feb 4, 1854</small>

The case of the *Trident* was that of a suit brought against that vessel, a steamer, by the sailing barge the *Southampton*, on account of a collision which took place between them on the 7th May, 1853, about 11.30 P M.

The *Trident* was coming down the River, and the *Southampton* was in Bugsby's Reach crossing from the Essex to the Kentish shore.

It appeared in evidence that there was no light on board the *Southampton*, and the first question, therefore, was— whether this neglect of compliance with the Admiralty Regulations deprived her of her right of proceeding against the other vessel, to recover recompense for the damage sustained in consequence of the collision

The Court, addressing the Trinity Masters, observed that the Act of Parliament directs that a light shall be hoisted, when it is necessary, on board sailing vessels. It also states that the person whose duty it is to hoist a light shall not recover if the collision was occasioned by the omission to do so If you are of opinion that the collision was occasioned by the omission, then it is evident, whatever may be the other merits of the case, the *Southampton* cannot recover. The Trinity Masters expressed their opinion that the collision was not occasioned by this neglect, and that on other grounds the steamer was in fault. The Court condemned her in the damages

The *Mora Castle* was a case of collision between that vessel and the *Thomas and Ann*, which occurred between them about 7 30 P M. of the 25th October, 1854, off Dungeness. *March 2, 1855.*

It appeared in evidence that the *Thomas and Ann* was laid-to to wait for better weather, and that a light was placed over the starboard side of the bowsprit

The Court, addressing the Trinity Masters, observed, that it was for them to determine whether, considering that the place in which the *Thomas and Ann* was, a crowded fairway, they had a proper light, and added that, as they admitted they saw the other vessel half a mile off, they might have got out of the way of the brig. The Trinity Masters expressed their opinion that the collision was occasioned by the misconduct of the *Thomas and Ann*, and the Court pronounced against her.

The case of the *Bessie* was one of collision between that vessel and the *Norton*, in Bridlington Bay, on the 8th December, 1854, about 2 A M. *May 18, 1855.*

The latter vessel was at anchor, and the case turned upon the point whether she had exhibited a light at all, and if so, whether in a proper manner. The balance of the evidence in the opinion of the Court was, that a light was exhibited, but that it was not exhibited at the masthead, according to the Regulations of the Lords of the Admiralty, but in the fore rigging

The Court observed, that being in the fore rigging it would be clear of the rigging, and that the case was thus distinguished from that of the *Telegraph*, in which case, in the opinion of the Judicial Committee, the light was hoisted in such a position that vessels approaching from a given quarter could not ascertain there was a light at all.

The Trinity Masters being of opinion that although the light was not hoisted as directed by the Lords of the Admiralty, yet that it was so hoisted that it did give due notice to all vessels approaching her, and that it was impossible to say that the collision was at all occasioned by the light being put in the fore rigging instead of being at the masthead, the Court pronounced in favour of the *Norton*, condemning the *Bessie* in the damages.

S. G
July 2,
1855

In the case of the *Clyde*, before referred to, p. 36, and in which an action was brought against that vessel, a steamer, by the schooner the *George and Eliza*, it appeared in evidence that no light was exhibited by the schooner, and the question was whether such omission had contributed to the accident

The Court, after having commented on the Regulations, as mentioned before, added, the Act of Parliament does not go on to say that in all cases where there has been an omission to comply with its terms, the vessel shall not recover, but it is said that if the omission to show a light should occasion the collision, in that case the party shall not recover, and the question I would put to you, addressing the Trinity Masters, is in these words Are you of opinion that if the schooner had shown a light the steamer would have discerned her sooner, and also the course she was going, and in consequence thereof might have taken such lawful nautical measures as would have prevented the collision? if so, then the schooner could not recover.

After a short consultation the Court expressed their unanimous opinion to be, that the collision was occasioned by the improper steering of the steamer, and that though no light was hoisted, yet that the schooner was seen in time for the steamer to have avoided the collision if proper measures had been adopted. They thought it possible that had a light been hoisted the attention of the steamer might have been directed to it, and other measures pursued, but did not consider that possibility as coming within the meaning of the Act of Parliament, so as to say that the schooner, by not hoisting a light, not only violated the Act of Parliament, but occasioned the collision.

The Court therefore pronounced in favour of the schooner, and condemned the steamer in the damages

In the case of the *Vivid*, before referred to, the collision took place on the 11th August, 1855, about 11 30 P M, off Dover Harbour, where the *Henry* had been brought up The *Vivid* was a steamer employed in carrying the mails to Dover, and was proceeding at the rate of 12 miles an hour.

April 18, 1856.

It appeared in evidence that the *Henry*, whilst so at anchor, had hung a signal lantern on a spar under the boom of the foresail, about four feet on the starboard side of the foremast, and about twenty feet above her bulwark.

With respect to the position of the light, the Court observed, that it was admitted that the Admiralty Regulations had not been complied with, and the question then resolved itself into that of what is the effect of non-compliance with these Regulations.

If nothing had been said in the Act of Parliament except

simply that such lights should be hoisted according to those directions, it would have been impossible for any man to have maintained a suit who had disregarded compliance with them, the legislature had, however, guarded against that consequence by another section in the Act, and had in effect said this, you shall not be estopped from bringing your action merely in consequence of a breach of the Rules of the Admiralty, but if it be shown that the collision was occasioned by the non-observance of the Rule, then you shall be estopped, and referring to the case of the *Telegraph*, in which the Judicial Committee had held that to disentitle the vessel proceeding from recovering, the collision must be clearly traced to a departure from the Rules,—the Court, addressing the Trinity Masters, proceeded to observe that the Court could not do better than put the question in a way similar to that in which it had been put in that case, and requested the opinion of the Trinity Masters, whether, placed as the light was stated in evidence to have been, it would have been less visible than if it had been hoisted at the masthead, in that case it would be impossible for the parties to recover. But if, on the contrary, they were of opinion that, though the Regulations had been departed from, the place where it was suspended was just as visible to any vessel approaching from the port of Dover, then the law said that if the collision arose from the fault of the other vessel, the vessel proceeding should not be prevented from recovering by reason of having neglected to comply with these regulations

The Trinity Masters expressed their opinion that the *Henry* had a suitable light hoisted, that the exhibition of the light, as proved in evidence, was as visible to the steamer so approaching her as if it had been hoisted at the masthead, and that the collision was not occasioned by the departure from the Rules of the Admiralty.

The Court pronounced in favour of the *Henry*, condemning the *Vivid* in the damages; and this sentence was affirmed on appeal; their Lordships being of opinion that a light was exhibited on board the *Henry*, and must have been seen by those on board the *Vivid*, if a good lookout had been kept.

July 7, 1856.

In the case of the *Legatus*, a suit was brought against that vessel by the smack *Change*, on account of a collision which occurred between those vessels in the Lowestoff Roads, about 7 A.M 3rd November, 1855

May 19, 1856

It appeared in evidence that the smack was riding at single anchor, and had no light hoisted in compliance with the Admiralty Regulations, but on the part of the *Legatus* it was admitted that a vessel could be seen at the distance of half a mile

The Court, in addressing the Trinity Masters, observed, that although it had not been pleaded that the *Change* had exhibited no light, the Court was bound to take notice of that fact in consequence of the Act of Parliament.

The question, however, was whether or not the collision was occasioned by the absence of a light, and that such was not the case in any degree was clear from the evidence of the master of the *Legatus*, that he saw another vessel half a mile distant, though she had no light

The Trinity Masters concurred in opinion with the Court, that the *Legatus* was entirely to blame in not adopting the necessary measures to avoid the collision, and condemned that vessel in the damages.

Whittle v *Crawford*

July 4, 1856

This was originally an action tried at the Assizes at

Liverpool, on account of a collision between the brig *Exeter* and the barque *Northumbria's Daughter*, which occurred about 7 P.M. of the 7th April, 1855, in the Dover Roads, where the brig had brought up. It appeared in evidence that on being brought up a clear bright light had been hoisted by the mate of the brig on the fore boom, twenty-two feet from the deck, between the rigging and the mast, and that afterwards, about 9.30 P.M., the barque, in full sail, came in collision with her, and caused the damage

In defence, it was alleged on the part of the barque that the accident was attributable to the neglect of those on board the *Exeter*, in not having in compliance with the Admiralty Regulations exhibited the light at the masthead.

Mr. J. Crowder directed the jury that if they thought the collision was occasioned wholly or in part by the non-observance by the *Exeter* of the Regulations, as to placing a light on the masthead, the defendant, the owner of the barque, was entitled to a verdict; but that in his opinion all the evidence went strongly against such a conclusion, as the witnesses on both sides stated that the light at the boom of the foreyard was sufficient to enable the barque to avoid the collision. The jury gave a verdict against the barque; the defendant, her owner, moved the Court for a new trial, and on refusal appealed to the Exchequer Chamber. The judges rejected the appeal, and expressed their opinion that the judge in the Court below had directed the jury in the words of the statute, and that such direction was right.

The *Adonis* was a case in which the *Sir Robert Peel*, a Norwegian brig, proceeded against that vessel, a steamer, on account of a collision which occurred between them near Shoebury Ness, at the mouth of the River Thames, about 3 A.M. of the 2nd January, 1854

There was much discrepancy in the evidence respecting the state of the night; on the part of the brig, it was alleged that it was fair and clear, and that she had descried the steamer at the distance of three miles; on that of the steamer, on the contrary, that it was dark about the horizon, and by her the accident was in part attributed to the *Sir Robert Peel* not having shown, as it was admitted she had not, a light on descrying the steamer.

The Court having observed that the *Sir Robert Peel* being a foreign vessel, it was a question how far in this case she could be considered bound by the enactment of a British Act of Parliament, and noticed the discrepancy in the evidence, expressed its opinion that, independently of the Act, the night was such as to render it a reasonable precaution that the *Sir Robert Peel* should have shown a light, according to the common nautical usages and customs of the sea, and that neglect to do so might, even according to these principles, deprive her of a right to recover compensation. Assuming, however, the Act to apply, and the obligation thus expressly imposed upon her, it proceeded to observe, that there could not for a moment exist a doubt that the Act of Parliament was not verbally complied with, except the light was placed at the masthead; but the Act of Parliament did not rest there, it went on to say that compensation should not be recovered if the collision were occasioned by a breach of the Rule. It was therefore an important question in this case for the Trinity Masters to determine, whether if a light had been shown in due time after the discovery of the steamer by those on board the *Sir Robert Peel*, they were of opinion the collision would have been avoided or not—in other words, whether the non observance of the Rule did occasion the collision.

The Trinity Masters expressed their opinion, that although the *Sir Robert Peel* ought to have shown a light, the collision was not occasioned by her having omitted to do so, that the *Adonis* saw her in ample time to avoid her, and that the collision was occasioned wholly by the neglect and erroneous conduct of the steamer.

The Court pronounced in favour of the *Sir Robert Peel*.

Neglect of Rule occasion of the collision.

IN THE FOLLOWING CASES, on the contrary, it has been held that there had been such neglect as to deprive the parties of their remedy.

1 Sp 96
Nov 21,
1853.

The *Aliwall* was the case of a collision between that vessel, a brig, and the *Ann Moore*, another brig, which occurred off Flamborough Head, on the night of the 10th January, 1853.

It appeared in evidence that the night was dark, and that there was much difficulty in discerning objects at a distance.

Neither vessel had complied with the Admiralty Regulations, enjoining them, on approaching or being approached by any other vessel, to show a bright light.

The Court referring to the Regulations, and that they were qualified by the condition annexed, that no recompense should be recovered in case it should appear that the collision was occasioned by the non-observance of them, left it to the Trinity Masters to decide whether in this case the collision was occasioned by not hoisting a light, and, as they were of opinion that lights ought to have been hoisted by both vessels, decided that both parties were precluded by the § 28 from recovering damages.

14 & 15 V.
c. 79, p 18.

1 Sp 298
May 7,
1854.

The *Fairy* was a case of collision which took place off Cromer, about 8 o'clock P.M. of February 26, 1853. The vessel proceeding against her was the *Kirton*.

Although the subject of *Lights* was not touched upon by the counsel on either side, as it appeared in evidence that none had been exhibited by either vessel, the Court felt it a matter of duty to bring the subject to the notice of the Trinity Masters,

Such neglect, according to the principles applicable to to these actions, being of a nature to deprive any vessel of the right to sue another

The Court, referring to the Act of Parliament, expressed its opinion that the *Kirton* ought to have exhibited a light as soon as she descried the other vessel approaching, and it therefore became necessary to consider whether the non-exhibition of the light was the cause of the collision.

The Trinity Masters expressed their opinion that it was the duty of both ships to have shown a light, that if this had been done there would have been no collision, and therefore the neglect to show a light was the cause of it.

The Court held the *Kirton* to be thus deprived of the right of action, and therefore dismissed the suit.

In the case of the *Telegraph* before cited, p. 30, the effect of non-compliance with the rules came fully before the Court. [1 Sp 427. May.]

On the part of the *Palermo*, the other vessel with which the collision took place, it was proved that the light had been hoisted in her larboard mizen rigging instead of at the masthead

The Court observed on the non-compliance on the part of the *Palermo* with the Regulations, and added, addressing the Trinity Masters, the next inquiry will therefore be, what are the legal consequences of not having literally complied with the statute, and these are, that such neglect shall preclude the parties guilty from recovering the loss sustained in any collision where it shall appear that such collision was occasioned by the non-observance of that rule.

The question submitted by the Court to the Trinity Masters was, whether the *Telegraph* proceeding from the port of Belfast would be able to descry a vessel with the same facility with a light hoisted at the larboard mizen rigging as she would if it had been at the masthead; should they be of opinion that she would not, then it might be fairly inferred that the collision might have been avoided by hoisting a light at the masthead, and that it was occasioned in consequence of it not being so hoisted. If, on the other hand, they were of opinion that in all probability the light would be equally discerned at the larboard mizen rigging and at the masthead, then it would be impossible to say that the collision was occasioned by a disregard of the terms of the Act.

The Trinity Masters being of opinion that under all the circumstances the light was more visible at the larboard mizen rigging than at the masthead, the Court pronounced for the damages in favour of the *Palermo*.

On the appeal, however, before alluded to, p. 30, the Judicial Committee was assisted by two gentlemen who were sailing masters in the Royal Navy, and Sir J. Paterson, in delivering the judgment, observed that that Court quite agreed with the learned Judge of the Admiralty Court in the views which he took with respect to many points of the evidence, and with respect to the general law which he laid down on the subject, and after having, in the terms already cited, observed that the *very top* was the place for the light according to the Regulations, added, that in this case the *Palermo* was anchored with her head to the south, about S SE, or thereabouts, and the wind was blowing against her head; the proper course of the steamer being E. by N., she would come to the starboard side of the vessel; but the light being in the larboard mizen rigging, the sailing masters by whom the Court was assisted differed in opinion from the Trinity Masters who assisted the Court below, and were of opinion that the light in the larboard mizen rigging would not be as visible as one at the masthead to a vessel approaching as the *Telegraph* did on the larboard side, but might have been hidden from view.

The inference therefore was, that the collision was occasioned by a breach of the regulations, and the Court therefore reversed the judgment.

The question of the non observance of the Regulations also came before the Court of Queen's Bench before Lord Chief Justice Campbell, Thursday, June 28, 1854, in the case of *Dixon* v. *Clement and others*.

June 29, 1854.

This was a case of collision between two collier vessels, neither of them having exhibited a light, in conformity with the Regulations.

In summing up to the jury the Chief Justice, after having commented on the Regulations and the great importance of a strict attention to them, observed that the first question he would ask them was whether those on board the *Abeona*, the plaintiff's vessel, were guilty of a breach of the Regulations, and that it contributed to the loss—not, was the sole cause of the loss, but that it contributed to it, that it occasioned the loss within the meaning of the Act of Parliament.

The jury found a verdict for the defendants on the ground that the *Abeona* had not exhibited a light, and that such neglect had contributed to the collision.

In the case of the *Temiscouata*, that vessel was proceeded against by the *Lawrence*, a sloop, on account of a collision

Oct. 26, 1854.

which took place between them off Spurn Point, at the mouth of the Humber, about 4 A M. of the 26th September, 1854.

Both vessels had been compelled to come to anchor by stress of weather, the wind blowing a gale from the N.W, and the night most tempestuous, and so dark that it was almost impossible to see a vessel at a greater distance off than its own length The anchors of the *Temiscouata* would not hold her and she began to drive, when the collision took place between them.

Both parties had lights, on board the *Lawrence* it was fastened to the starboard rigging, and on that of the *Temiscouata* on the foreyard.

With respect to the question of the light on board the *Lawrence*, the vessel proceeding against the other, the Court observed, that unquestionably it was not placed as was directed by the Act of Parliament. That Act requires it to be fastened to the masthead, whereas it was fastened to the starboard rigging. The question therefore was, whether the fact of this lantern being appended to the starboard rigging instead of at the masthead was the occasion of the collision, and whether, if it had been appended to the masthead, it would have made any difference in the case, and this question was to be considered with reference to the wind and the sea, and that the light, whatever it was, was observed.

The Trinity Masters were of opinion that the collision in no degree arose in consequence of the light not having been hoisted at the masthead, that the *Temiscouata* had not taken the proper measures to avoid the collision, and the Court condemned her in the damages.

Dec 24, 1855

The *Juliana* was a case in which that vessel was proceeded against by the trawl-sloop the *Fearnot*, on account of a collision which occurred on the 29th November, 1854, about 9 P.M, off the Eddystone lighthouse.

It appeared in evidence that the night was a clear night, not particularly clear or dark, that the *Juliana* had a light clearly exhibited, but that on board the *Fearnot* there was none shown; it was also proved that they had descried the other vessel about a quarter of a mile distant.

The Court observing upon the importance of the Act of Parliament bearing on that subject, and the necessity of a strict attention to it, quoted at length the § 298; and, as it was admitted that the *Fearnot* had not complied with the Regulations of the Admiralty respecting lights, proceeded to examine how far such neglect could be said to be the occasion of the collision in the latter words of that section, adding—We all know that such a night requires the exhibition of a light when you see a vessel approaching. How are we to try the probabilities of this case supposing that a light had been exhibited? If a light had been exhibited under the circumstances, does it not almost amount to a certainty that those on board the *Juliana* would have seen the fishing sloop in time, and would have avoided her? Then what is the other conclusion to which the Court must come? If the exhibition of a light would have prevented a collision, why the non-exhibition of it was the occasion of the collision. Of that I can entertain no doubt, and the gentlemen by whom the Court is assisted are of opinion with myself that the action cannot be maintained I do hope that this amongst other instances may be a warning to all concerned in shipping matters, that they must attend to the provisions of the Act of Parliament. If they do not, and vessels are run down, they can neither recover in this Court nor any other

17 & 18 V. c 104, p.18.

The suit was therefore dismissed with costs.

May 5, 1856.

The *Neptune* was a suit between that vessel, a steamer, and the *Unity*, a sloop, in which cross actions were brought against one another by both vessels on account of a collision which took place between them at 5.15 P.M. of the 10th November, in the river Tyne.

The *Unity* was being towed by a steam tug, but was, as it was admitted, without a light.

Upon this point the Court, addressing the Trinity Masters, observed that with regard to the *Unity* not showing a light, it was clearly of opinion that she was bound to have shown one, the words of the Regulations are specific and perfectly intelligible. Another consideration was whether the not showing a light was in any degree the cause of the collision, or contributory thereto, whether, if a light had been shown in due time, it might have given warning to the steamer and have induced her to have taken other measures, which would have prevented the calamity.

The Trinity Masters having pronounced their opinion that the *Neptune* was to blame in not porting her helm, but that the *Unity* was also in fault for not hoisting a light in due time, and that such neglect was a contributory cause to the collision, the Court decreed that neither party was entitled to recover.

May 19, 1856.

The case of the *Queen Dowager* was one in which a suit was brought against that vessel by the brig the *Friends' Increase*, on account of a collision which took place between them about 2.30 A.M of the 4th February, 1856, off Scarborough.

It appeared in evidence that the night was dark and hazy, that the master of the brig having observed a light at a little distance, went below for a light, and the same was immediately exhibited, but on the part of the *Queen Dowager* it was contended that this exhibition of the light did not take place until she had approached within fifty yards of the smack, and that such neglect was the occasion of the collision, and therefore deprived her of all right of suing for compensation.

The Court, addressing the Trinity Masters, observed that the question which it appeared necessary to put was this— Whether the master ought not, considering that the night was dark and hazy, and looking at the terms in which the directions given by the Lords of the Admiralty are couched, to have had a light ready; and whether he was not chargeable with that delay which brought him within the words of this order, that a sufficient light should be shown in time to avoid the collision.

The Trinity Masters expressed their opinion that the brig was to blame in not hoisting a light at an earlier period; that it might have been possible, if the light had been so hoisted, that the other vessel might have taken warning; but that the collision was occasioned by the *Queen Dowager* not porting her helm in time.

Both parties were in fault, and the damages therefore were directed to be divided.

The *Gulnare* was a case of collision between that vessel and the Prussian brigantine *Lucinde*, which occurred in the Bristol Channel about 8 30 on the 3rd January, 1854, in which cross actions were brought against each other.

May 26, 1856.

It appeared in evidence that it was a very tempestuous night, that the *Lucinde* had two lights up, hung on the mainstay before the foremast, but the *Gulnare* had none; and that the *Lucinde* had descried that vessel at the distance of about a quarter of a mile

The Court, in addressing the Trinity Masters, observed that, with respect to the lights of the *Lucinde*, the simple question was, whether they were so hoisted as to give warning to other vessels approaching, and there was no doubt they were, for it was admitted on all hands that they were seen. With respect to the *Gulnare*, it added the expression of its firm conviction that she was to blame for not having hoisted a light, and that, independently of the Act of Parliament, on such a night it was her bounden duty to have shown one. Having neglected to do so, it then became a question how far such neglect occasioned the collision, and deprived her of a right to recover damages. It was for them to say whether, if the *Gulnare* had shown a light the moment she descried those of the *Lucinde*, the collision might not in all probability have been avoided, as, if she had hoisted a light, she might have been seen sooner, and thus there would have been more time for the *Lucinde* to have got out of the way.

The Trinity Masters expressed their opinion that the *Gulnare* was alone to blame, and particularly in not showing a light; and that no blame attached to the other vessel.

The Court pronounced against the *Gulnare*.

Jurist, 1856. 2 N S p 620 June 14, 15.

The case of the *Mangerton* was that of an action brought by the owners of the *Josephine Willis* against the *Mangerton* in consequence of a collision which took place between these two vessels, and by reason of which the latter vessel and the lives of many of the crew and passengers were lost.

It appeared in evidence that the *Josephine Willis* had fastened at the end of the bowsprit a triangular-shaped lantern, showing by means of lenses three lights; a bright light in the front, a green light on the starboard, and a red light on the port side.

In the course of the argument the question was raised, whether such a light was a compliance with the Admiralty Regulations established in pursuance of the 14 & 15 V., c 79, and whether these regulations themselves had not been suspended by later enactments, by which that statute was repealed.

The Court held that these Regulations still remained in force, observing that the Merchant Shipping Act of 1854, together with an Act that immediately passed afterwards, the Merchant Shipping Repeal Act, 17 & 18 V., c. 120, repealed all former statutes, but these particularly excepted. Now, what is the exception? "Any byelaws or regulations subsisting when the Act came into operation." And upon these words the Court expressed its opinion that the meaning was, that the Regulations do prevail which were in force prior to 1854, but that the Lords of the Admiralty should have the power of revoking them and establishing new Rules.

<small>17 & 18 V., c 120, § 4, par. 7.</small>

<small>See p 20</small>

Upon the former point it was of opinion that the light exhibited was not conformable with the Admiralty Regulations, and, as the omission to do this contributed to occasion the collision, decreed that the *Josephine Willis* was not entitled to claim compensation for the injury sustained.

IT HAS BEFORE been stated that the modifications in general maritime law, introduced by legislative enactments and regulations founded upon them, can only apply to the case of those parties who may be subjects of the powers by whom such regulations have been made, or who may have placed themselves within their jurisdiction.

The extent of that jurisdiction has been held in general to extend over the territory of the country itself and three miles[1] from the coast, and includes ports and harbours, and, generally speaking, bays along the coast.

WHERE BOTH vessels between which the collision takes place are the property of British subjects, Regulations founded upon the enactments of a British Act of Parliament are applicable to the case, in whatever part of the world the accident may have occurred, whether within British waters or at a distance on the open ocean

With cases of the first description, viz, where the collision has taken place within British waters, the Reports abound As instances, amongst the cases before cited, it will be sufficient to refer to that of the *Swanland*, in which the collision took place in the Humber, and to that of the *Bessie*, in which the vessels, the subjects of the action, came into collision in Bridlington Bay

v p 40.
p 45.

The other cases of collision without the territorial jurisdiction and on open sea, although not so frequent, are by no means of rare occurrence Of these, an instance occurs in the case of the *Benares* before cited, and where the collision took place at sea, in lat. 6° 7' N., and long. 19° 42' 30" W

p. 9.

WHERE, HOWEVER, ONE OR BOTH of the parties are foreigners and not resident within the jurisdiction, a question may arise how far they are bound to observe the regulations of a government from whose authority they are exempt, as owing to it no allegiance.

PREVIOUS TO the examination of the question, a few observations on the jurisdiction exercised in the case of foreigners generally will not be misplaced.

---

[1] Vide *Vrow Anna Catharina*, 5 Rob. 17; also 3 Hay, 289.

The Court before which questions relating to maritime matters, such as collision, salvage, &c, are generally brought, is naturally that of the High Court of Admiralty. From its constitution it is one of General as well as British Maritime Jurisdiction, and the power it possesses and in practice generally exercises, of proceeding *in rem*, and arresting any ship which may come within its juridiction to answer to a suit brought against it, is one which points it out as almost exclusively the Court to which recourse would be had when proceedings are intended against a vessel, the property of foreigners and which, after the occurrence of the cause of action, may by any chance have come within the British Jurisdiction.

The cases in which foreigners may be parties are divisible into the three following:

1. Where a British subject proceeds against a foreign vessel.
2. Where a foreigner proceeds against a vessel belonging to British owners.
3. Where both parties are foreigners.

WITH RESPECT TO the case of British subjects proceeding against a vessel the property of foreign owners, which may have come within the jurisdiction of the High Court of Admiralty, their right is unquestionable and its exercise of almost daily occurrence.

The right of proceeding in that Court, in cases in which a foreigner was concerned, was brought before it in the case of the *Two Friends*.[1] This was an American vessel, which had been rescued from the enemy and brought into an English port by its crew, part of which consisted of British seamen,

[1] 1 Rob. 271.

who were merely working their passage home, and as salvors had commenced proceedings in the Court of Admiralty

Although this was a case of salvage, the reasoning of the Court upon which its judgment was founded, was of so general a nature as to be applicable to most cases of Admiralty jurisdiction

A preliminary objection had been taken to the jurisdiction of the Court, 1st, because the ship was an American ship, and 2ndly, because the claimants, as it was contended, were to be considered American sailors.

The Court, however, immediately set aside the second ground of objection, pronouncing its opinion that under the circumstances the claimants were clearly to be considered British subjects, and with respect to the general question of the right of American sailors to proceed against American property in that Court, in a case of salvage, although it then became unnecessary to determine it, it pronounced a strong opinion in favour of such a right, observing that salvage was a question of the *jus gentium*, a general claim upon the general ground of *quantum meruit*, to be governed by a sound discretion acting on general principles; and it could see no reason why one country should be afraid to trust to the equity of the Court of another on such a question of such a nature so to be determined, adding that there was great reason for the exercise of its jurisdiction, as being the only way of enforcing the best security—that of the lien on the property itself, and continued, that if there were British property on board an American ship rescued from the enemy, and American seamen were to proceed as salvors in the Court of Admiralty against that, it would consider it a criminal desertion of duty if it did not support their claim

And accordingly pronounced in favour of the English seamen to sue in that Court.

Other instances of proceedings on the part of English owners against Foreign vessels are the following.

The *Eolides* This was the case of a Swedish ship proceeded against by a British vessel, the *Royal Oak*, for injury done to her whilst at anchor in the Thames, and in which the Court condemned the Foreign vessel in the damages. 3 Hag 367.

The *IX Martz* was a cause of damage, in which the owners of the British brig *Carnation* sought to recover the loss sustained in a collision with the Prussian vessel *IX. Martz*, near Copenhagen. 7 Ca. 371.

After examining the evidence on both sides, the Court decided that the blame was attributable to the *Carnation*, and therefore dismissed the Foreign vessel

IN THE SAME MANNER our Courts of Justice are open to any foreigner who may have sustained injury from a British vessel which has returned to this country, provided the country of such foreigner is not engaged in hostilities with Great Britain. For it is a general rule that in all cases, save as to real estate, an alien friend is entitled to sue on the same footing as a British born subject.

The foreigner, however, in such a case, is required to give security for costs as being out of the jurisdiction. 1 Ca. 444.
6 Ca. 166

Thus, in the case of the *Clyde*, that was a suit promoted by the Danish schooner the *Catherine Ferdinand* against the steamship *Clyde*, to recover compensation for damage arising from a collision off Flamborough Head. 2 Sp 27
Oct. 20,
1854.

The Court pronounced in favour of the Foreign schooner

F

<small>1 W Rob 316 Jan 22, 1842</small>

The *Vernon* was also the case of an action brought against that vessel, an East Indiaman, by the owners of the *Alsen*, a Norwegian barque, on account of a collision which occurred between these ships near Dungeness, but in which the Court held that, although the injury was the act of the vessel proceeded against, that vessel was exonerated from the consequences under the Pilot Act, as the blame rested entirely with the pilot in charge of her, and under these circumstances the owners of the vessel were relieved from all responsibility

ACTIONS MAY ALSO in some cases be brought in the Admiralty by foreigners against one another

These, however, are only in cases which naturally fall under the *jus gentium*, such as salvage, collision, &c.; in other cases, such as wages, which may depend upon the construction of a mariner's contract, a creature of the particular institution of each country, to be applied, construed, and explained by its own particular rules, the Court is reluctant to interfere,[1] and in general will only do so with the consent of the representative of the nation to which the parties belong

<small>1 W Rob 38.</small>

IN THE MATTER OF COLLISION, this subject was brought fully before the Court in the case of the *Johann Friedrich*.

In that case proceedings were commenced by the owners of the Danish vessel *Delos* against the *Johann Friedrich*, the property of citizens of Bremen.

The collision took place between Dover and Dungeness, the consequence of which was the total loss of the *Delos*. The *Johann Friedrich* after the collision put into the port of Ramsgate, and while there was arrested under a warrant

---

[1] *Martin of Norfolk*, 4 Rob 297 *Courtney*, Edw, 240 *Vrow Mina*, 1 Dod 134

from the High Court of Admiralty. Bail was given, and an appearance entered on the part of her owners under protest to the jurisdiction of the Court, on the ground that both vessels being the property of foreigners, and the accident having occurred on the high seas, the matter was not legally cognizable by this Court

The Court, observing upon the peculiar nature of the action and the inconvenience which would attend its refusal to entertain it, as, if the parties must wait until the vessel that had done the injury returned to its own country, their remedy might be altogether lost, or, in the event of her return home, there was no part of the world so distant, to which they might not be sent for their redress, overruled the protest, and pronounced in favour of its jurisdiction on the following grounds:

1. That all causes of collision are *communis juris*.
2. That the vessel, at the time of her arrest, was within the Admiralty jurisdiction.
3. That the collision took place on the high seas, close upon the English coast

But in such cases the Court will require the party proceeding to give security for costs, in the same manner as in the case of a suit by a foreigner against a British subject. [1 W. Rob. 39.]

AFTER HAVING THUS STATED what was the position in our Court of a Foreign vessel which had had the misfortune to come into collision with another vessel, British or Foreign, previous to the first regulation laid down under the authority of the 9 & 10 Vict., c. 100, the next question is to consider what has been the effect of other and subsequent regulations on vessels of that description

This question has been on one or two occasions indirectly referred to, and it appeared that the opinion of the Court was to consider such regulations as clearly not applicable to any case in which a Foreign vessel was a party, *where it was not proved that the collision occurred within three miles of the coast.* Thus, in the case of the *Ericson*, which was that of a suit promoted against that vessel, an American steamer, by the British barque *Alderman Thompson*, on account of a collision which occurred between them off Dover, about midnight on the 15th October, 1855.

On the part of the American vessel, it was contended that the British barque was in fault in the course they adopted, as, according to the Act of Parliament, they ought to have ported their helm and got out of the way.

The Court, addressing the Trinity Masters, observed—The American vessel, I will assume for a moment, was within what are called "British Waters," I will assume that at the moment she would have been subject to the laws of Great Britain, but I assume it because, in the first place, it is not proved to me that she was within three miles of the coast; secondly, I reserve to myself, in case of need, the question whether, when a Foreign vessel is within three miles of the coast, she would or would not be subject to the provisions of that statute, but assuming that she was, the Court considered the construction of the Act contended for on the part of the *Ericson* an erroneous one, and, as in the opinion of the Trinity Masters the American vessel was to blame for not keeping a good look-out, condemned her in the damages.

The *Dumfries* was a case of collision between that vessel, a British barque, and the Danish schooner *Christina Maria*, on account of a collision on the high seas off Whitby

In addressing the Trinity Masters, the Court observed

that in this instance they were relieved altogether from the consideration of what was the true construction to be put on the Act of Parliament, which was so often brought under their notice, because this being a case on the high seas, between a Foreign and a British ship, it appears to me, unless overruled, that we cannot apply the Act of Parliament, but the case must be governed entirely by ordinary nautical rules.

The case of the *Robert Watson*, was that of a suit promoted by the American ship *Chapin*, against that vessel, a British barque, on account of a collision which occurred between them off the *Newfoundland* coast, on the 2nd September, 1854.

March 10, 1855.

In the course of the argument, reference was made to the Act of Parliament enjoining the manner in which vessels are to pass one another.

In addressing the Trinity Masters, the Court observed, that in this case the Act of Parliament had no application, because one of them was an American vessel, and it would never bind one vessel down by the Act of Parliament, while the other was at liberty to go free; the case must, therefore, be considered according to the ordinary principles of nautical science.

This question, however, was directly brought before the Court for its decision in the case of the *Zollverein*, which was that of a collision between the British brig *Pet* and the Foreign vessel *Zollverein*, which occurred off Flamborough Head, about 3.30 of the 12th November, 1855; and in which proceedings were commenced by the British vessel against the Foreign ship, to recover damages for the total loss of the former in consequence of the accident.

Ap 25, 1856.

The Trinity Masters, who assisted the Court on the

hearing of the cause, were of opinion that, according to the general principles of maritime law, the *Pet* was justified in the conduct she pursued of keeping her course; but, according to the regulations established by the § 296[1] of the Merchant Shipping Act, she ought to have ported

The question, therefore, came before the Court to determine whether, under the § 298, she was barred by such non-observance from recovering recompense for the damage sustained in the collision, and led to an examination how far the enactments of a British Act of Parliament were applicable to the case of collision between a British ship and a Foreign vessel on the high seas, where the Foreign vessel had commenced proceedings against the British vessel in the English Court of Admiralty.

17 & 18 V, c 104, p 19.

The Court, in giving its judgment, observed that the power of this country was to legislate for its own subjects all over the world and as to foreigners within its jurisdiction, and that it would be very slow to think that any attempt had been made to exceed this power, unless the words of the statute were so express as to deprive it of the capability of concluding to the contrary. And although the words were so ample as to embrace every ship British or Foreign, sailing on the ocean, they must be construed with

Merchant Shipping Act, 1854 17 & 18 V, c 104, § 296

[1] "Whenever any ship, whether a steam or sailing ship, proceeding in one direction, meets another ship, whether a steam or sailing ship, proceeding in another direction, so that if both ships were to continue their respective courses they would pass so near as to involve any risk of a collision, the helms of both ships shall be put to port so as to pass on the port side of each other, and this rule shall be obeyed by all steam ships and by all sailing ships, whether on the port or starboard tack, and whether close hauled or not, unless the circumstances of the case are such as to render a departure from the rule necessary in order to avoid immediate danger, and subject also to the proviso that due regard shall be had to the dangers of navigation, and, as regards sailing vessels on the starboard tack close hauled, to the keeping such ships under command "

due reference to what must be considered as the intention of the legislature, as far as their right and power extended, to control foreign ships

Referring to Judge Story's Conflict of Laws, ch. 14, § 558, the learned Judge cited the following passage:—

"In regard to the merits and rights involved in "actions, the law of the place where they originated is to "govern, but the form of remedies, and the order of judicial "proceedings are to be according to the law of the place "where the action is instituted;" and observed that the question was, when a collision takes place on the high seas between a British vessel and a Foreign ship, by what law should such a case be tried, if a suit be brought in the English Court of Admiralty So far as regards the Foreign ship, the answer is, that it must be tried by those rules of navigation which usually prevail among maritime nations navigating the seas, when the collision takes place. The Foreigner cannot be supposed to know, neither is he bound by the municipal laws of Great Britain, or any other state purporting to regulate the conduct of vessels belonging to it, on the high seas If the Foreigner commences the suit before the tribunals of this country, then, so far as extends to the remedy, he must abide by the law of the country to whose tribunal he may resort In other words, the merits of the collision must be tried by the Law Maritime, independent of statutes The remedy must be according to the *Lex Loci*—the tribunal resorted to.

The Foreigner being thus freed from all observance of a British Act of Parliament, equity would require that the other vessel, although British, should be equally released from all observance of it.

The Court expressed its opinion that the whole of the § 296 did apply strictly to the merits of the case, and to the question how the vessels shall conduct themselves at the time of the collision, and that a Foreign vessel therefore would not be bound by the regulations contained therein,[1] they were therefore equally inapplicable to the British vessel, and therefore decided in favour of the *Pet*.

SINCE THE PASSING of these Acts, several instances of collision have also occurred with and between Foreign vessels in "British waters." Under that denomination a distance of three miles from the coast is included, the territorial jurisdiction of a country being considered to extend to the distance of a marine league, or about three miles from the shore, the distance to which in former times it was supposed a cannon ball would reach [2]

The general principle of law is, that cases of wrong are to be decided according to the law of the place where the wrong is committed, and this principle appears to have been admitted in the Courts of the United States of America in cases of collision: thus in the case of *Smith* v. *Condry*, which was carried on appeal to the Supreme Court of the United States, a collision had taken place between the vessels of the plaintiff and defendant (both American), in the port of Liverpool, in this country, the Court below were of opinion that the vessel of the defendant was in fault, but that the accident was attributable to the pilot in charge: that the collision having taken place in a port of Great Britain, the rights of the parties depended upon the provisions of the British

---

[1] *Don* v *Lipman*, 5 Clarke and Finelly, p 1, cited in the *Vernon*, 1 W Rob 319

statutes then in force there, their construction being that which is sanctioned by the Courts of that country; and as the British Court of Admiralty had on several recent occasions held that, under the Pilot Act, 6 Geo IV., c 125, a party was not responsible for damages occasioned by the fault of the pilot in charge of the vessel, the defendant in this case was entitled to the same exemption, and this decision was affirmed.

Upon the same principle foreign vessels are held to be bound by the local regulations of ports and harbours into which they may come, and by those of the Custom-house

In the cases, however, just alluded to, as it is the duty and interest of the parties to make themselves acquainted with the regulations established by the laws of the countries they visit, there is every reason to believe they are fully cognizant of them; and this observation might, perhaps, also be applied to the case of foreign vessels in the habit of frequenting "British Waters" It is evident, however, that there might be great difficulty in identifying such vessels, and that ignorance of any national regulations might justly be pleaded on the part of vessels accidentally approaching the coast,[1] or possibly driven in by stress of weather

[1] Hefter, p 148

The Court of Admiralty in this country, in the several cases of collision between a British and foreign vessel, or two foreign vessels, which have been brought before it, has decided that a British statute was not applicable to them Thus, in the case of the *Active*, which was a case of collision between that vessel (a foreign barque) and the British brig *Alert*, off Whitby, the Court observed, "This being a collision between a foreign and an English ship, we have nothing to do with the Act of Parliament· we may leave it out of consideration, and our judgment must be go-

Jan 30, 1857

See also Christiana, Jan 14

verned by the ordinary rules of navigation among civilized nations

April 21, 1856

The *Borussia* was a case in which the *Therese*, a foreign barque, proceeded against that vessel, a foreign steamer, to recover compensation for an injury sustained in a collision which took place between them in the Hull Roads, where the *Therese* had brought up

On the part of the *Borussia* the accident was attributed to the *Therese* not having a proper light suspended.

Erroneous, see new A.R. 95

The Court, addressing the Trinity Masters, observed, "We must bear in mind that we are speaking of foreign vessels which had arrived within the waters of Hull, and if the *Therese* recovers it will not be by the English law, but by the maritime law of the world." and, the Trinity Masters having expressed their opinion that the *Borussia* had not been misled by the lights, although they were defective, condemned her in the damages

AFTER WHAT HAS BEEN STATED in the previous pages, and the decisions of the Court in the cases which have been referred to, the present state of the law respecting the use of "Lights," may be summed up in few words

ALL BRITISH VESSELS are bound among themselves to observe the Regulations established by the Lords of the Admiralty under the authority of Parliament

These Regulations enjoin the use of a bright light by all vessels when at anchor, to be exhibited by sailing vessels at the masthead

That steam vessels at other times, when under steam, should exhibit a bright white light at the foremast head in a lantern so constructed as to show a uniform light over an arc of the horizon of 20 points, 10 on each side of the ship; a green light on the starboard, and a red light on the port side, the lanterns in which they are shown being so constructed as to show a uniform light over an arc of the horizon of 10 points, viz, from right ahead to 2 points abaft the beam on the respective sides. These lanterns are to be fitted with screens on the inboard side of at least three feet long, to prevent the lights being seen across the bow

The light at the masthead to be of such power as to be visible at a distance of at least *five* miles, those on each side at a distance of at least *two* miles.

And that all sailing vessels, when under sail or being towed, approaching or being approached by another vessel, should in the same manner, between sunset and sunrise, show a bright light where it best can be seen, and in time to avoid collision.[1]

WITH RESPECT TO FOREIGN VESSELS, these regulations are held not to apply to them.

No case appears to have yet occurred in which the Court has been called upon to express an opinion on the effect of ordinances established by a Foreign Government, of a similar tendency[2] with the Regulations adopted in our own country

SINCE THE PRECEDING PAGES WERE WRITTEN, another commission has been issued for the further examination and re-consideration of this question, and reporting upon the most desirable and practicable mode of exhibiting lights at sea.

By this Committee many witnesses have been examined, and much valuable information obtained

---

[1] Vide Regulations of 1852, p 21
[2] Wheaton, Int L, pt. 2, c 2   *Fortune*, 1 Dod 84

Their report bears date March 29th, 1856, and concludes with the following recommendations :—

Firstly,—That no alterations should be made in the present system of steamers' lights.

Secondly,—That the bright light now exhibited by sailing vessels, when under sail or being towed, should be abolished, and that instead thereof such vessels should exhibit, between sunset and sunrise, to any vessel or vessels a Red light on the port side and a Green light on the starboard side, corresponding to the coloured side-light now shown by steamers without any reference to tacks.

Thirdly,—That these coloured lights should be fixed when practicable; and that when such lights are not fixed, places should be provided in which the lights should be kept on their respective sides ready for exhibition.

Fourthly,—That all lights, whether fixed or exhibited by hand, should be so screened as to render them invisible on the opposite bow or side of the vessel, which the Committee consider quite practicable.

Fifthly,—That the lights proposed to be exhibited by sailing vessels should in no case be of less size or power than the lantern which the Committee recommend, and which shows an uniform and unbroken light over sixteen points of the compass.

Sixthly,—That all vessels at anchor, whether steamers or sailing vessels, should exhibit, "where best seen," between sunset and sunrise, a White light, of uniform size and power, in a globular lantern of six inches in diameter, at a height not exceeding twenty feet above the hull of the vessel.

Seventhly,—The Committee consider it desirable further to recommend that the Pilot Vessels of the United Kingdom should be designated by particular lights. They would, therefore, submit that, in addition to the Red and Green lights now proposed for all classes of sailing vessels, Pilot vessels should be permitted to exhibit a White light on a level with the Red or Green light

Eighthly,—The Committee having taken into consideration the subject of signals during fogs, would recommend, for the reasons stated in the foregoing Report, that steamers should use either the steam-whistle or bell, and that all other vessels should use a fog-horn.

Finally,—The Committee are of opinion that the above regulations, if approved of by their lordships, should apply to all vessels of the United Kingdom in every part of the world, unless specially excepted by the Admiralty.

The Committee cannot close their report without stating that the evidence adduced proves that the number of collisions is chiefly attributable to the neglect of a "good look out," and they submit that it should be strongly impressed on the Masters of all vessels, that this important duty be more rigidly attended to.

THE RULE OF THE ROAD.

IN CLOSE CONNEXION with the subject of the preceding pages, and, like it, the object of customary rules and statutory enactments, is the law of Collision, particularly that part of it which relates to what is known as "the Rule of the Road," or the manner in which ships should pass one another at sea.

In the earlier stages of navigation, the necessity of the case obliged the different nations engaged in maritime commerce to adopt some common rules and regulations, which were confirmed by custom, and gradually formed, as it were, a kind of International Code

This, until a very recent period, was found sufficient to regulate their mutual intercourse with one another.

Of these rules, the principal are as follows —

1 A Vessel in motion is bound, if possible, to steer clear of and avoid a vessel at rest, and placed in such a situation that she cannot help herself

2. When the two vessels are close-hauled on different tacks, that on the starboard tack shall keep the wind, and the one on the larboard tack give way

3 A vessel going free should give way to a vessel close-hauled, the latter continuing on her course

4 When both vessels have the wind free, they should each port their helms

1 A VESSEL IN MOTION is bound, if possible, to steer clear of and avoid a vessel at rest, and placed in such a situation that she cannot help herself

Nov 22, 1851.

Thus, in the case of the *Hebe*, that vessel came into collision with the *Helena* off the coast of Spain, the latter vessel lying-to at the time, and, as was pleaded, motionless in the water

The Court observed, that if the *Hebe* was lying motionless in the water, it meant that she was unmanageable, and could do nothing to move herself out of the way, and if such were the case, and the other vessel could clearly distinguish her condition, and did not take proper steps to avoid her, she would be to blame

THIS RULE is frequently applied to the case of vessels at anchor being run into by other vessels in motion, vessels under these circumstances being in general so situated as to render it impossible for them to get out of the way.

Jan. 8, 1853.

Thus, in the case of the *Adventure*, that vessel and the *William Broderick* had been driven by stress of weather to anchor in the Yarmouth Roads The *William Broderick* was lying by her small bower anchor, and had afterwards let go her best bower anchor, when the *Adventure* drove from her anchor and came into collision with her

The Trinity Masters, by whom the Court was assisted, expressed their opinion that the *William Broderick*, not being at single anchor, but, as it were, pinned down, could do nothing; that the *Adventure* was in fault, as she ought to have given out more cable, let go her second anchor, and run up her topmast-staysail; and the Court accordingly condemned her in the damages

3 Hag 367

The *Eolides* was a case in which that vessel, whilst at anchor, was run foul of by the *Royal Oak*

The Court observed, that of two vessels, one under sail and the other at anchor, there was no question that it was the duty of the former to avoid the latter, and condemned the *Royal Oak* in the damages.

In the case of the *Volcano*,—that vessel, in H. M.'s service, came into collision with the brig *Helen* in a bay on the coast of Spain.

3 Ca. 210.

The latter vessel had already anchored in the bay, when the *Volcano*, compelled by stress of weather to take refuge there, came to anchor at two cables' length from the *Helen*, with her small bower anchor alone, several other vessels having also anchored there.

In the course of the night a hurricane arose, and caused the *Volcano* to drift, the anchor broke, and, although a second anchor was dropped, a collision took place between the vessels, the consequence of which was that the *Helen* was lost.

The Court expressed its opinion that there was a want of proper caution, on the part of the *Volcano*, in taking up her position in the first instance, and not being securely anchored, and afterwards in not letting out more cable and letting go a second anchor, and condemned her in the damages.

THE APPLICABILITY, however, of this rule to the case of vessels at anchor depends upon their inability to do anything to avoid the collision, and the presumption on that account is always in favour of a vessel so situated.

Thus, in the case of the *Harlequin*, the Court observed that where a vessel is lying at anchor, or in a harbour, it was impossible to say she was the cause of a collision, or to impute blame to her, as if she had been a vessel at sea.

May 23, 1856
v. p. 86.

WHERE, HOWEVER, it is in the power of the vessel at

anchor to take any steps to prevent the accident, and she neglects to do so, she will be held responsible for the neglect.

<small>May 13, 1854.</small>

Thus, in the case of the *Beaver*, a collision occurred in the Yarmouth Roads between that vessel (a brig) and the schooner *Barnard Castle*, about 11 A.M. of February 27th, 1853

Both vessels were bound to the north, and were at anchor when the *Beaver* parted from her cable and ran into the *Barnard Castle*

On the part of the *Barnard Castle*, it was contended t the *Beaver* ought to have let go a second anchor on rting from the first, and on that of the *Beaver*—that the breaking of the cable arose from stress of weather, and that the collision, therefore, was the result of inevitable accident,—that it would have been useless to let go a second anchor, as the vessels were so close to one another,—and that the fault was that of the *Barnard Castle*, in giving her foul berth

The Court, addressing the Trinity Masters, by whom it was assisted, observed, that where a vessel lying at anchor is run against by another vessel in motion, it lies upon that vessel which so comes into collision with the vessel lying at anchor to explain why and wherefore the collision took place, because, *primâ facie*, a vessel lying at anchor cannot be supposed to be to blame The blame may depend upon various atters it may be said that the collision was the result of inevitable accident, of a foul berth having been taken up by the vessel so run into, or that the vessel at anchor did not adopt, on her part, the measures within her power to avoid the collision

The Court then expressed its opinion that the collision

here was not the result of accident, and left the consideration of the case to the Trinity Masters, more particularly as to whether the *Beaver* ought not to have let go the second anchor, and whether, as it was the duty of the *Barnard Castle* to have done all in her power to avoid the collision, she ought not to have ported her helm, veered out more cable, and brought her head to the E, by which, in all probability, the collision would have been avoided.

They having expressed their opinion that both vessels were in fault in these respects, the Court decreed, accordingly, that the damage should be divided between them.

The *Temiscouata* was a case of collision between that vessel and the sloop *Lawrence*, which occurred about 4 A M. of the 26th of September, 1854, off Spurn Point, at the mouth of the Humber

Ante, p. 55
19 Jur.
479

Both vessels had been compelled to come to anchor by stress of weather; the wind was blowing a gale from the N.W., and the night most tempestuous.

The *Lawrence* had anchored off the Spurn Point, having two anchors down, a larboard and a starboard cable, the one at full length, the other about two parts let out, and previous to the collision had paid out five fathoms of her starboard cable.

The *Temiscouata* had drifted from her anchor, and run into the other vessel.

The Court observed, that the question with respect to the *Lawrence* was, whether that vessel was right in paying out the cable, and whether she ought and could have slipped from her anchors, or have done more in any way whatever; and with respect to the other vessel, whether she could have adopted any measure, with reference to her sails or otherwise which would have enabled her to avoid the collision, or whether it was the result of inevitable accident; and being of opinion that the fault was that of the *Temiscouata* in not having taken all the proper measures, the Court condemned her in the damages.

Nov. 20, 1839

In the case of the *Earl Bathurst*, that vessel, driven by stress of weather, came into collision with the *Adelaide*, which was anchored near the entrance of Milford Haven. The *Adelaide* had veered out all its cable when collision appeared to threaten it, but without success

The Court was of opinion that the *Adelaide* had done all she could, and that the other vessel was in fault, and condemned her in the damages.

V. p 72.

In the case of the *Kron Prins Ernst Auguste*, that vessel, sailing in company with the *Ide*, came suddenly to anchor, and a collision took place between them.

The Court, having expressed its opinion that the *Kron Prins* had brought up so suddenly that there was no means of avoiding the collision, and had also neglected to exhibit lights, condemned her in the damages.

IT IS HARDLY NECESSARY to observe, that it is incumbent upon all vessels to anchor in a proper place and proper manner, and the question whether they have done so has accordingly frequently been brought before the Court, in defence of the vessel proceeded against, for injury done to one in such a position.

The Court has, however, invariably expressed its opinion that such a defence was not admissible when the vessel in motion had the means of discerning the situation of the other vessel, and could have avoided her.

March 28, 1852

The *St. Columba* was a case in which that vessel, a steamer, was proceeded against by the schooner *Thetis*, on account of a collision which occurred between them when near the Platters Buoy in the Holyhead Roads.

The *Thetis*, it appeared in evidence, whilst on a voyage from Liverpool to Great Yarmouth, had been compelled to come to anchor by stress of weather. The night was dark and hazy, and vessels could only be seen in close proximity.

The *St Columba* alleged, on her part, that previous to the collision she had slackened her pace, and on descrying the other vessel had ported her helm, but discovering that the *Thetis* was at anchor the order was given to ease, stop, and reverse her engines; before, however, the influence of this was felt she came into collision with her. she also contended that the *Thetis* had improperly anchored in the fairway-track, and was thus herself the cause of the accident.

The Court, addressing the Trinity Masters, observed, that in this case it was quite sufficient for the *Thetis* to prove that she was lying at anchor, because, though she may be passively culpable, she could not be actually to blame; and then it became incumbent for the vessel proceeded against to show that she was not in fault Her defence was, first, that the *Thetis* was not in proper anchorage ground; if this were true, then undoubtedly that vessel would be to blame. but upon coming to a conclusion upon this point, they must consider the state of the wind, and other circumstances which might have rendered it expedient to stop at the place in which she did; they must also bear in mind, that, lying in an open roadstead such as the roads of Holyhead, was a very different thing from lying in a narrow sea or river, and with respect to the speed of the steamer, although she had slackened it, it was for them to consider, whether, looking at the circumstances of time and place, she ought not to have been so navigated as to be in a situation so as to avoid all danger of collision.

The Trinity Masters expressed their opinion that the *Thetis* was brought up in proper anchorage ground, but that the speed of the steamer was not sufficiently slackened in time. The Court accordingly condemned that vessel in the damages

May 23, 1856

Again, the case of the *Harlequin* was one of collision between that vessel, a steamer, and the steam-tug *Accommodation*, which took place about 9 A.M. of the 12th April, 1855, in the river Yare, at Yarmouth

The *Accommodation* was lying lashed alongside the *Cyrus*, which was moored outside another vessel, and was struck by the *Harlequin* after she had entered the river.

On the part of the *Harlequin*, it was contended that the accident was attributable to the improper position of the other vessel.

With reference to this, the Court showed that, supposing this to be so, supposing a vessel at anchor in an improper place, or a carriage on shore to be placed in an improper position, the law is clear that if you can with proper and ordinary skill without doing damage to yourself or others, avoid a collision, it is your duty so to do, and if you do not you are responsible.

The Trinity Masters having expressed their opinion that the *Harlequin* might thus have avoided the collision, the Court condemned her in the damages

4 Ca 356

The case of the *Batavier* was one of collision between that vessel and the *Topaz*, it appeared in evidence that the latter had, on the morning of the day on which the accident occurred, had come out of dock and was at single anchor nearly opposite, 200 or 300 feet from the Essex shore, between it and the Whiting sand, when the *Batavier* attempting to pass her, going to eastward, a collision occurred between them

The Court, addressing the Trinity Masters, by whom it was assisted, expressed its opinion that the *Topaz* was not anchored in an improper place, nor, considering the circumstances, in an improper manner, and that the *Batavier* had not pursued a proper course in going to the N E of the other vessel, observing that it was the duty of a vessel to avoid if possible, without danger to itself, a collision with another vessel at anchor, even if anchored improperly and in an improper place, but added, that, although the *Batavier* was to blame, the fault was that of the pilot in whose charge she was, and therefore her owners were relieved from the responsibility

In the case of the *Gipsey King*, the *Highlander* having been ashore, but afterwards floated and riding at single anchor without being moored, was run foul of by that vessel.

5 Ca. 282

The Court expressed its opinion, that under the circumstances it was allowable for the *Highlander* to lie a tide or two at single anchor without being moored, and that the *Gipsey King* was to blame, but held her to be exonerated from responsibility, the accident having arisen from the fault of the pilot on board

In the case of the *Troubadour* and *Lance*, the latter vessel was anchored in Milford Haven, when the former, entering that port to take up passengers, came into collision with her, and attributed the accident to the *Lance* having anchored in an improper place

Ap. 17, 1852

The Court, however, expressed its opinion that such was

not the case, adding, if it was impracticable to enter the harbour without running down the vessel, the *Troubadour* had no right to enter at all

IN SOME CASES the accident has occurred between two vessels, which have both been at anchor, and one of them has drifted or for some other reason got into motion; thus in the case of the *Adventure*, before cited, p. 29, and in that of the *Northampton*, in which that vessel and the *Feronia* had both anchored off Liverpool, when the former vessel, having dragged her anchor, came into collision with the latter; on the part of the *Northampton*, it was contended that the *Feronia* had given her foul berth, but on that of the *Feronia*, that the accident was occasioned by the neglect of those on board the other vessel to send down their top-gallant yard and strike that mast, and veer out more cable

1 Sp. 52.

The Court, having noticed the distinction between dragging an anchor and driving, added, "The river was lying N. and S. When the vessel swung to her anchor, her head would be to the S. Now, if by reason of the force of the tide she had drifted down the river from her anchor, that is driving; but if her anchor had gone after her, she would both have drifted and dragged her anchor." And, with reference to the charge of the *Feronia* having given the *Northampton* foul berth, observed, that "when two vessels anchor, there should be that space left between them for the swinging to the anchor that in ordinary circumstances the two vessels cannot come together; if that space is not left, I apprehend it is foul berth"

The Trinity Masters, by whom the Court was assisted, were of opinion that the *Feronia* was not in foul berth, and that it was advisable for the *Northampton* to have sent down her yards and mast, but that the collision was occasioned by her dragging her anchor, which might have been prevented by letting go another anchor. This, however, being the fault of the pilot, the Court held the *Northampton* to be exonerated from responsibility.

In the case of the *Ernest*, that vessel and the *Rambler* had both come to anchor; the former began to drive, and was not brought up until she came to within half a cable's length of the latter. The anchor of the *Rambler* was fouled by that of the *Ernest* crossing her cable, and on the turn of the tide the vessels came into collision.

April 28, 1853.

The Court pronounced the *Ernest* to be in fault.

In the case of the *Christiania*, that vessel and the *Marshal Bennett* had both come to anchor in the Downs, when the former vessel, in consequence of her having been run against by another vessel, drove from her anchor and came into collision with the *Marshal Bennett*.

7 Ca 2

The Court expressed its opinion that the latter vessel was not in fault, but that the *Christiania* was to blame; that she might have been brought up after she had been run into, if she had not previously neglected to have sent down her yards, and accordingly condemned her in the damages.

In the case of the *Spray*, that vessel, drifting up the river in company with the *Hannah and Eleanor* and two other vessels, was compelled to come suddenly to anchor, in consequence of the other vessels preceding her having done so. The *Hannah and Eleanor*, a short distance astern on the starboard quarter, was therefore hailed by her to let go an anchor, and, on being thus brought up, the vessels came into collision.

May 10, 1856

The Court observed that the question would in the first place be, whether the *Spray* might not have avoided the collision by starboarding her helm, whether she had given due, *i.e.*, sufficient, notice to the *Hannah and Eleanor* to enable that vessel to take the necessary steps, and then whether that vessel did all that she could, and expressed its opinion that the *Spray* was alone in fault.

June 22, 1853. In the case of the *Catherine*, that vessel and the sloop *Liberty* had both come to anchor, when the former, having recommenced her voyage, run foul of the other, and was condemned in the damages.

June 11, 1856. In the case of the *Lidskjalf*, that vessel had brought up alongside of the *George*, which had anchored for the purpose of discharging her cargo; on the fall of the tide the former vessel listed against the latter, and did her considerable damage.

The Court, having observed that when a vessel is lying on the shore, and another vessel is placed voluntarily in such a position that damage will happen if some event arises which it is not possible to control, this second vessel must be responsible for such damage, pronounced the *Lidskjalf* to be in fault.

UPON THE SAME PRINCIPLE of the impossibility of their being able to get out of the way, this rule has been held applicable to vessels in positions similar to those at anchor, as when at moorings.

3 Hag 160. In the case of the *Girolamo*, that vessel ran foul of the *Edward*, a British convict ship moored off Woolwich.

The Court observed that the vessel in motion and governable was bound, if possible, to steer clear of and avoid a vessel at her moorings, and nothing could in such a case excuse her from making compensation but unavoidable accident, and condemned the *Girolamo* in the damages.

In the case of the *Cyrus*, that vessel and the *Homer* were both moored at the entrance of the Regent's Canal Docks, waiting to enter, when, on the dockmaster having given the necessary directions for that purpose, they came into collision

The Court was of opinion that the *Homer* was to blame, having given the *Cyrus* foul berth, and condemned her in the damages

April 20, 1855

AGAIN, WHEN the vessel run into is "lying to."

In the case of the *Six*, that vessel, on the starboard tack, came into collision with the sloop *Wilson*, whilst she was lying to on the larboard tack.

May 26, 1852.

The Court observed that the first question was whether the *Wilson* was lying to, as if not, being on the larboard tack, it was her duty to get out of the way, and then if she were lying to, whether she was justified in doing so, as in that case, if the *Six* was enabled to discover in due time it was her duty to avoid her, not merely by porting her helm, but by giving way altogether, because no vessel is justified in coming into collision with another if she can keep away by any reasonable means, but expressed its opinion that if the *Wilson* were lying to she was not justified in doing so on account of the weather, which had been very tempestuous, and the crowded state of the thoroughfare, and therefore pronounced in favour of the *Six*.

In the case of the *Afrika*, that vessel was proceeded against by the *Stirlingshire*, on account of a collision which occurred between them whilst the latter was lying to under close-reefed main-topsail, about ten miles to the S of Portland

June 17, 1856

The Court expressed its opinion that the *Stirlingshire* was to blame in lying to in the immediate track of vessels, without having proper sail to keep her under command, and dismissed the suit.

1 Sp 288

In the case of the *Blenheim*, that vessel, being laid to with her head N by W (the wind W by N), reefing her topsails, and helm hard a starboard, came into collision, off Flamborough Head, with the *Unition*, bound for Jersey, close-hauled on the starboard tack.

The *Blenheim*, although she saw the light on board the other vessel, did nothing

The Court, being of opinion that the *Blenheim* might and ought to have ported her helm, condemned her in the damages.

June 6, 1853

In the case of the *Vesta*, that vessel, close-hauled on the starboard tack, came into collision with the fishing-smack *Osprey*, whilst the latter was lying to on a wind on the larboard tack, and, after having descried the other vessel, took no further steps to avoid the collision than exhibiting a light.

The Court pronounced the *Osprey* to be in fault, and dismissed the suit

July 3, 1857.

In the case of the *Sir Thomas Stanley* and the *Wizard*, the collision took place in the river Mersey; the wind was S S.W. The *Sir Thomas Stanley*, a steam-tug, was proceeding with a loaded flat to discharge her cargo into the *Sir W Eyre*, lying at anchor in that river, and was preparing to lie off till the turn of the tide, and, on the approach of the *Wizard*, reversed her engines, but to no purpose. The *Wizard* was crossing the river in an easterly direction on the starboard tack, and on approaching the steam-tug, having hailed her to no purpose, starboarded her helm, when the collision took place.

The Court, being of opinion that the *Wizard* ought to

have tacked before there was any risk of collision, and that it was owing to her reckless conduct, condemned her in the damages

In the case of the *Cyrus* and *Mary*, the latter vessel, about 3 A.M of the 27th April, 1856, when a little off Flamborough, had hove to to pick up some French sailors whose vessel had just sunk, and was, as she stated, out of command. The *Cyrus*, having perceived the *Mary* at the distance of a quarter of a mile, had taken no steps to avoid the collision till too late, and attributed the accident to the *Mary* not having observed the Admiralty Regulations, and hoisted a light. April 4, 1857.

The Court, having observed that the Admiralty Regulations requiring lights only applied to vessels at anchor in a fairway, and not to such a case as this, and being of opinion that the *Cyrus* was solely in fault, condemned her in the damages

In the case of the *City of London* and the *Celerity*, an action was brought by the latter vessel against the former to recover damages for injury resulting from a collision between them on January 3, 1857; the night was clear and moonlight. The *Celerity*, a fishing smack, was hove to for the purpose of reefing one of her sails, and had not exhibited any light; the *City of London*, a steamer, having four persons on the look out, not perceiving the *Celerity* through the glare of the moonlight, came into collision with her June 6, 1857.

The Court expressed its opinion that the *Celerity*, although hove to, was still to be considered a sailing vessel, and, as such, fell under the enactment of the § 298 of the Merchant Shipping Act, and was bound to have exhibited a light, and that the collision was occasioned by such neglect, and, therefore, that she could not recover damages from the other vessel, and dismissed the suit

<small>June 13, 1855</small>

OR THE VESSEL, which is run foul of by the other, may be in the act of "putting about, in stays, &c, &c."

In the case of the *Mariner*, a collision took place between that vessel and the *Margaret Molcolm*, the latter vessel being put about on the port tack, and, on the approach of the other vessel, her yards kept aback

The Court observed, that the position in which the latter vessel was contended to have been, was one in which she was incapable of doing anything, somewhat similar to a vessel at anchor; and, undoubtedly, if she had been seen by the *Mariner* in that state, and it was possible for that vessel to have avoided the collision, she ought to have done so; but, not being of opinion that such was the case, the Court pronounced the *Mariner* to be free from blame

<small>Nov. 18, 1859</small>

In the case of the *Presto*, a collision occurred between that vessel and the *Ann*.

Both vessels were crossing the river, and the *Ann* was being put about to avoid collision with another vessel, when she was run into by the *Presto*.

The Court expressed its opinion that the *Ann*, being in stays, was free from blame; but that the *Presto* ought to have tacked before she came to her.

<small>July 18, 1855</small>

In the case of the *Teresita*, a collision occurred between that vessel and the *Alert* The former vessel was tacking, and, at the time, in stays; the *Alert* was sailing with the wind free

The Court, being of opinion that the *Teresita* had a right to expect that she could tack with safety, and that the *Alert*, although she did port her helm, ought to have ported it sufficiently to keep clear, condemned the latter vessel in the damages

In the case of the *Elizabeth Mary Anne*, a collision took place between that vessel and the schooner *Mary Ann*. Both vessels were close hauled on the starboard tack, and the former vessel astern of the other, which came into stays for the purpose of changing her tack, when the accident occurred.

May 20, 1854.

The Court observed, the question was, whether the *Mary Ann* was in stays, and if so whether she was properly so; that it appeared from the evidence that vessels might be seen two miles off; she, therefore, ought not to have gone about if there was any danger in so doing. If, however, she was properly in stays, the other vessel was to blame for running down a vessel that could not help herself; but, being of opinion that she was not in stays, pronounced against her.

In the case of the *Royal Consort*, that vessel, close hauled on the larboard tack whilst in stays, came into collision with the *Brilliant*, which was at a distance of about six cables, when she was going to put about.

Nov 6, 1851.

The Court observed that the question was, whether under these circumstances the *Royal Consort* might and could have put about, and have recovered her course so as to avoid the collision, and, being of opinion she could not, condemned her in the damages.

In the case of the *Kingston by Sea*, a collision occurred between that vessel and the *Thirsk* packet.

Feb 1, 1849.

The *Kingston by Sea* had tacked and missed stays when the collision took place

The Court observed, that that vessel had the power to choose the distance at which she should tack, and that if a vessel is put in stays and misses, it is her duty to square the main yard, when she would pay off; and being of opinion that the *Kingston by Sea* was in fault, condemned her in the damages

OR THE VESSEL may have grounded.

<small>Jan 22, 1853</small>

In the case of the *Mary Maria*, the brig *Friends*, having taken the ground aft on the Blythe Sand, canted round and remained fixed there, when she was run into by the schooner *Mary Maria*. The Court being of opinion that the *Mary Maria* was to blame, and that she ought to have gone about in time, condemned her in the damages.

IN SOME RESPECTS, also, fishing vessels are assimilated to vessels at anchor, but not so as to render them liable to the enactment of any statute which may have passed with reference to the latter

In the case of the *Two Sisters*, that vessel came into collision with the *Good Samaritan*, a fishing lugger, when the latter had shot her nets, and was riding by them.

<small>See also Napoleon III., ante, p 33</small>

The Court observed, that there could be no doubt that when a vessel is situated as the *Good Samaritan* was, viz, exactly the same as if she had been at anchor lying to her nets, so that there was an impossibility of helping herself if another vessel came into contact with her, the burden of proof lay on that other vessel to show that she could not avoid that accident, although she adopted every means in her power so to do, and, being of opinion that the *Two Sisters* was to blame, condemned her in the damages.

<small>Nov 27, 1852</small>

In the case of the *Southampton*, that vessel sailing free came into collision with the fishing smack *Jane Burrow*, whilst the latter was engaged in fishing with the trawl net down, moving at the rate of half a mile an hour, and having the tiller detached from the rudder.

The Court being of opinion that the fishing smack under such circumstances could do nothing to cause the collision, and that the *Southampton* had not taken the proper precautions in time, comdemned that vessel in the damages.

In the case of the *Reliance* and *Hope*, the latter was dredging for oysters on the oyster grounds off Beachy Head, with two dredges down, when the *Reliance*, running down channel, came into collision, and sunk her.

June 6, 1857.

There was contradictory evidence with respect to the question whether the *Hope* had exhibited a light or not: on her part evidence was produced to prove that there was a light at the mainmast; viz., a lantern with three glasses, and an eight candle in it.

The Court, having alluded to the condition of the *Hope* with two dredges down, and consequently the difficulty of avoiding collision, and to the presumption in favour of the affirmative evidence that there was a light on board that vessel, expressed its opinion that the *Reliance* was in fault, and condemned her in the damages.

II WHEN THE TWO VESSELS are close-hauled on different tacks, the one on the starboard tack should keep the wind, and the one on the larboard tack give way.

In the case of the *England*, an action was brought against vessel by the *William Broderick*, on account of a collision which occurred between them on the morning of the 8th August, 1844, in the river St. Lawrence, the weather being thick and foggy.

5 Ca. 175.

The wind was westerly, both vessels were proceeding up the river, the *England* on the larboard tack, the *William Broderick* on the starboard.

The Court, addressing the Trinity Masters, by whom it was assisted, observed, that the rule was that when two vessels are on a wind, that on the larboard tack is to give way to the one on the starboard tack; if there is a reasonable chance of collision this rule applies, whether the vessel be to the windward or to the leeward, but, of course, not where there is no chance of collision, when each vessel keeps its course Vessels, however, are not to speculate upon the matter whether the vessel was a little to the leeward or to the windward, but to obey the rule even in broad daylight.

The Trinity Masters, however, in this case were of opinion, that, from the state of the weather, the vessels, when first seen, were so close that the collision was inevitable, and the Court therefore dismissed the suit.

3 Hag. 320

In the case of the *Jupiter*, that vessel, on the larboard tack, came into collision with the *William Wilberforce*, the latter vessel being on the starboard tack, both beating to windward The *Jupiter* bore up, to allow three sail to pass to windward, the *Wilberforce* ordered her helm a-weather.

The Court observed, here are two vessels beating to windward on contrary tacks; the *Wilberforce* was on the starboard tack, and should therefore, according to the well-known rule, have held on her course, but she began wearing There was no doubt that she was to blame

Jan 31, 1839

In the case of the *Aline*, that vessel, coming down channel close-hauled on the starboard tack, on the 22nd of September, 1838. came into collision with the *Panther*, which was going up channel close-hauled on the larboard tack

The Court, having expressed its opinion that the *Aline* was in fault in having her helm down, as, being on the larboard tack, she ought to have had it up, condemned her in the damages.

In the case of the *George*, an action was brought against 5 Ca. 368. that vessel on account of a collision which took place between that vessel and the *Globe* about 6 30 P M of the 18th of December, 1846.

The *Globe* was proceeding from Stockton to Topsham, having the wind three points free, and, perceiving the other vessel at a distance of about a quarter of a mile, kept her course; the *George* was close-hauled on the larboard tack, ported her helm, and, squaring her sails, kept before the wind.

The Court observed that, it being dark, the Trinity rule did not apply; that the rule undoubtedly was, that when two vessels approach each other, no matter on what tack they may be, the one that has the wind free ought to give way, and the other not to alter her course to avoid damage on either side; but the question was whether, when two vessels are meeting at night, and it is impossible to ascertain whether the vessel is close-hauled or not, the vessel on the larboard tack close-hauled ought not to port her helm, as well as the vessel on the starboard tack.

The Trinity Masters, by whom the Court was assisted, were of opinion that the *Globe* was to blame, even if she had only two points of the wind free, she ought to have ported her helm, and that the master of the *George* acted right.

The Court accordingly dismissed the suit. Affirmed on 6 Ca. 56. appeal.

In the case of the *Test*, a collision took place between 5 Ca. 276. that vessel and the *Mayflower* on the morning of the 20th of November, 1846.

Both vessels were bound to the southward, and were both close-hauled, the *Mayflower* on the starboard and the *Test* on the larboard tack; the latter vessel, having observed the *Mayflower* at a distance of a quarter of a mile, hailed her to give way, but without effect

The Court observed that it was the duty of the *Test* to have given way; and the Trinity Masters having expressed their opinion that she had time to wear up if she had put up the helm when first she saw the *Mayflower*, considered her to blame, and the Court condemned her in the damages.

6 Ca 36. In the case of the *Stranger* and *St. Petersburgh*, the former vessel was close-hauled on the larboard tack, and the latter on the starboard tack

The Court observed that, according to the general rule of a vessel on the larboard tack giving way to one on the starboard tack, it was the duty of the *Stranger* to have given way, to have put her helm hard a-port, haul down the foresail, ease the main-sheet, and lower the peek, and not having done so, the blame was solely attributable to her.

May 6, 1853. In the case of the *Gipsey King* and *Pomona*, a collision took place between these vessels whilst close-hauled on different tacks, neither vessel having taken any steps to avoid the collision.

The Court observed, that, admitting the correctness of the rule that it was the duty of the vessel on the larboard tack to give way, and that on the starboard tack to keep her course, yet if it were possible for the latter vessel to have done anything by which the collision could be avoided, it was her duty to have done it, and expressed its opinion that both vessels were to blame: it therefore directed the united loss to be divided between them in equal portions in the usual manner.

1 Sp 186. In the case of the *Sea Park* and *Hendrike*, the latter

vessel was on the larboard tack close-hauled, and, on perceiving the latter vessel, ported her helm.

The *Sea Park* was steering E N.E, the wind being S. by E, and also ported her helm.

The Court expressed its opinion that the *Sea Park* was in fault, as she should have kept her course, and condemned her in the damages.

In the case of the *John Biddle* and the *Eliza Ann*, the latter vessel was on the starboard tack close-hauled, proceeding to the S, the former on the larboard tack proceeding to the N, but at the time occupied in reefing her sails, and, as contended, unmanageable, and unable to do anything. 5 Ca 387

The Court observed, that according to the ordinary rules the *John Biddle* ought to have given way, but that under the circumstances it was a pure accident, and that she was therefore free from blame.

In the case of the *IX. Martz* and the *Carnation*, the latter vessel was on the larboard tack, and to avoid the collision hove about. The former was on the starboard tack, and put her helm a-lee, but, missing stays, fell a-board the *Carnation*. 7 Ca 371

The Court, being of opinion that the *Carnation*, instead of attempting to go to windward of the foreign vessel, ought to have bore up in time, and given way, pronounced her to be in fault.

III. A VESSEL GOING FREE should give way to a vessel close-hauled, the latter continuing on her course.

In the case of the *Baron Holberg*, that vessel whilst going down the river with a westerly wind, came into collision with a barge beating up 3 H ag. 244.

The Court observed, that the *Baron Holberg* had complete command of the course, and that the rule was clear that a vessel with a free course must give way to a vessel beating up to windward and tacking

3 Ca. 13　In the case of the *Colonia*, a collision took place between that vessel and the *Susan* off Folkestone on the 4th October, 1844, in daylight, the weather being fine, the *Colonia* had the wind free

The Court observed, with reference to the timely precaution which a vessel ought to take, that the whole evidence showed that it was the duty of the *Colonia*, with the wind free, to have made certain of avoiding the *Susan*; she did not do so, but kept her course till she was at a cable and a half's length; that it never could be allowed to a vessel to enter into new calculations which must be attended with some risk, whilst it has the power to adopt, long before the collision, measures which would render it impossible, and condemned the *Colonia* in the damages.

3 Hag 322　In the case of the *Celt*, that vessel came into collision with the schooner *Anthony* The former vessel had the wind free; the latter was close-hauled on the starboard tack, working up the Irish Channel, and, in order to avoid the *Celt*, attempted to wear out of her way

The Court expressed its opinion that the *Anthony* was in fault, as, being close-hauled, she ought to have continued on her course, and not have attempted to wear, and accordingly dismissed the suit, but refused to allow the *Celt* her costs, on account of the inhumanity displayed in not assisting the crew of the other vessel after the collision.

Ca 584.　In the case of the *Immaganda*, that vessel, coming up channel on the larboard tack, going free, came into collision with the *New Forest*, close-hauled on the starboard tack, and at first kept her course, but afterwards (as contended on her part), to ease the blow, put her helm to starboard.

The Court observed, that according to all ordinary rules of navigation it was the duty of the *Immaganda* to have ported her helm and given way, and that of the *New Forest* to have kept her course or ported her helm; but as, on the contrary, she had put it to starboard, she was in fault.

On appeal, this decision was reversed, the Court considering both vessels to have been in fault. *Feb 19, 1852.*

In the case of the *Red Jacket*, that vessel was coming up channel perfectly free, her course being N.E; the *Emerald Isle* was going down channel close-hauled, and her course was N.N W, when they came into collision, the former vessel having starboarded her helm twice, and the latter having first put hers to port and then to starboard. *June 11, 1856.*

The Court expressed its opinion that, under the circumstances, the *Emerald Isle* was justified in expecting the other vessel to pass under her stern, and keeping close to the wind; the *Red Jacket* was to blame for not porting in time, and going under the stern of the *Emerald Isle;* and accordingly condemned the *Red Jacket* in the damages.

The *Finland* was a case of collision between that vessel, which was coming down channel with a perfectly fair wind, and the *Hope*, which was on the starboard tack close-hauled, bound up channel. *June 28, 1852*

It had been alleged in argument that the latter vessel was in fault, in not having taken any measures to avoid the collision.

The Court observed, that it was clearly the duty of the *Finland* to get out of the way, and, with respect to the *Hope*, added, that *primâ facie* a vessel close-hauled on the starboard tack is not bound to take immediate measures to avoid a collision; there may be exceptions to this rule, but then it must be proved that there were measures which she could adopt to avoid it, and, being of opinion that the *Finland* was alone to blame, condemned her in the damages.

2 Dod, 83. In the case of the *Woodrop Sims*, that vessel, having the wind free, came into collision with the *Industry*, steering a S W course close by the wind on the starboard tack.

The Court, having observed that the law imposes upon the vessel having the wind free the obligation of taking proper measures to get out of the way of a vessel that is close-hauled, and of shewing that it has done so, or otherwise that the owners are responsible for the loss which ensues, pronounced the *Woodrop Sims* to blame, and condemned her in the damages.

Jan 23, 1851. In the case of the *Sir George Seymour* and the *Victoria*, the vessels were approaching each other end on, the former vessel having the wind free, the latter being close-hauled on the starboard tack, they both, as stated, ported their helms.

The Court observed, that according to the general rule it was the primary duty of the *Victoria* to have kept her course, subjoined to this duty, however, was the duty of avoiding the collision, provided she could do so; and accordingly, under the circumstances, she ought to have ported her helm, which she appeared to have done, and was therefore free from blame; and added, that had the *Sir George Seymour* ported her helm, as contended on her part, and as was her duty, the collision could not have occurred. It considered that vessel, therefore, to be in fault, and condemned her in the damages.[1]

---

[1] Affirmed on appeal, Dec. 23, 1851

In the case of the *Athol* and *Jane Clark*, the latter vessel was proceeding down channel close-hauled on the larboard tack, the former running up with the wind free, also on the larboard tack, and, on perceiving the other vessel, first starboarded her helm and then put it to port.

1 Ca 586.
July 23, 1843.

The Court expressed its opinion that, from the evidence, it appeared that the vessels were coming end on, and under these circumstances, one sailing down channel on a wind and the other coming up with the wind free, it was the duty of both to port and go to larboard, that the *Athol* was in fault in having starboarded her helm in the first instance, and condemned her in the damages.

In the case of the *Benares* and the *Royal Archer*, the former vessel was on the starboard tack coming before the wind, and the latter on the larboard tack; the vessels were approaching one another in a direct line, when the *Benares* starboarded her helm; the *Royal Archer* ported hers, and let go the mizen-sheet.

7 Ca. 541.

The Court expressed its opinion, that the *Royal Archer* being on a wind on the port tack, it was her duty to have bore up as soon as she could discover which way the other vessel was going, and as she immediately ported her helm and eased off the mizen-sheet, she was free from blame; but that the *Benares* was wrong in not having immediately ported her helm, and condemned her in the damages.

In the case of the *Fortitude*, that vessel, proceeding down channel on the starboard tack with the wind free, came into collision with the *Condor*, which was proceeding on the larboard tack close-hauled; the latter vessel having kept her course till the danger was imminent, when she ported her helm.

June 23, 1851.

The Court observed that the common rule was, that when

a vessel is on the starboard tack with the wind free, it is her duty to give way to another vessel, although on the larboard tack, and although, if there be any danger of collision, the latter vessel is bound to do all she can to prevent the consequences, it does not follow that she is to give way in the first instance, and, being of opinion that the *Fortitude* was solely in fault, condemned her in the damages.

2 Ca. 476. In the case of the *Traveller*, that vessel, sailing on the larboard tack, came into collision with the schooner *Yarm* on the starboard tack, on the night of the 4th of January, 1843, both vessels kept their course, and on the part of the *Traveller* it was contended that she was justified in doing so, as the other vessel had the wind free.

The Court, however, expressed its opinion that at night it is the duty of a vessel sailing on the larboard tack to give way to a vessel on the starboard tack, though that vessel have the wind free, and condemned the *Traveller* in the damages.

5 Ca 375. In the case of the *Stadacona*, that vessel was coming down the Channel free on the larboard tack, and came into collision with the *Isabella* on the starboard tack; the latter vessel kept her course, and the former, after some time, ported her helm.

The Court expressed its opinion that the *Isabella* had done all she could, but that the *Stadacona* was in fault for not having ported her helm in time, and accordingly condemned her in the damages.

Nov 10, 1854. In the case of the *Fortitude*, that vessel, having the wind free, came into collision with the *Sir Robert Peel*, close-hauled on the port tack, about 3.30 A.M. of February 1, 1854, the night being dark and foggy.

The Court observed, that the *Fortitude*, having the wind

free, upon her lay the burthen of proof that the collision arose from circumstances beyond their control, and that all proper care and exertion had been taken on her part; that it was not simply the night being thick and foggy that would operate as an excuse, but being so thick and foggy that ordinary care would not have prevented the calamity, and being of opinion that she had not satisfied this proof, condemned her in the damages.

WHEN BOTH VESSELS have the wind free, they should each port their helm.

In the case of the *John Sugars* and the *Neptune*, both vessels had the wind free; the former, on observing the latter vessel, ported her helm; the latter asserted that she had also ported hers, but this was denied by the *John Sugars*, who accused her of having put it to starboard. July 16, 1853

The Court observed, that both having the wind free, as soon as they saw each other they should each have ported their helms; but it was of opinion that the *Neptune* had starboarded hers, and therefore was solely in fault.

In the case of the *Edward* and *Melisse*, both vessels had the wind free, the *Melisse* ported her helm and kept her luff, but there was no evidence to show what the *Edward* had done. 7 Ca 401.

The Court was of opinion that the *Edward* was in fault for not having ported her helm, and condemned her in the damages.

In the case of the *Superior* and *Zion*, both vessels had the wind free; the latter was coming up the river on the starboard tack, and starboarded her helm; the former was going down on the larboard tack, and put hers to port. 6 Ca. 610.

The Court expressed its opinion that the *Superior* had

followed the general rule of navigation, which the *Zion* had violated, and therefore that vessel was to blame:

SUCH WERE THE PRINCIPAL RULES which had been established, as it were by the common consent of nations, to regulate the navigation of the seas, previous to the introduction of steam vessels. shortly after they came into common use, the necessity of some more precise regulations, applicable to this class of vessels, was felt, and the Corporation of the Trinity House, as being in a more especial manner entrusted with the superintendance of British shipping, directed their attention to the recommendations it might be desirable to publish with respect to the navigation of these vessels, and accordingly, towards the end of the year 1840 they issued the following notice.

"NAVIGATION OF STEAM VESSELS.

"*Trinity House, London, 30th October*, 1840.

"The attention of this corporation having been directed to the numerous severe, and in some instances fatal, accidents which have resulted from the collision of vessels navigated by steam; and it appearing to be indispensably necessary, in order to guard against the recurrence of similar calamities, that a regulation should be established for the guidance and government of persons entrusted with the charge of such vessels; and whereas the recognised rule for sailing vessels is,

' That those having the wind fair shall give way to those on a wind:

"That when both are going by the wind, the vessel on the starboard tack shall keep her wind, and the one on the larboard tack bear up,—thereby passing each other on the larboard hand

' That when both vessels have the wind large, or a-beam, and meet, they shall pass each other in the same way on the larboard hand; to effect which two last-mentioned objects, the helm must be put to port.

"And as steam vessels may be considered in the light of vessels navigating with a fair wind, and should give way to sailing vessels on a wind on either tack, it becomes only necessary to provide a rule for their observance when meeting other steamers or sailing vessels going large. Under these circumstances, and with the object before stated, this Board has deemed it right to frame and promulgate the following rule, which, on communication with the Lords Commissioners of the Admiralty, the Elder Brethren find has been already adopted in respect of steam vessels in Her Majesty's service, and they desire earnestly to impress upon the minds of all persons having charge of steam vessels, the propriety and urgent necessity of a strict adherence thereto; viz,

"*Rule:*—When steam vessels on different courses must unavoidably or necessarily cross so near that, by continuing their respective courses, there would be a risk of coming in collision, each vessel shall put her helm to port, so as always to pass on the larboard side of each other

"A steam vessel passing another in a narrow channel must always leave the vessel she is passing on the larboard hand."

THESE RULES were brought to the notice of the Court in the case of the *Friends,* when the Court observed that the real substance of them was; 1st, To state certain 2 Ca. 92. recognised rules, not to enact them as rules, but to state them as rules which have long prevailed; 2ndly, without establishing any rule, it states what ought to be considered the power and condition of steam vessels, viz, that they should be considered as vessels going free. It then purports to provide a rule for their observance when meeting other steamers or sailing vessels going large; and with regard to its authority, it had previously observed in the case of the *Duke of Sussex*, that if any steam vessel, after it had been sufficiently promulgated, should neglect to comply with it, the Court will hold its crew guilty of unseaman-like conduct, and throw upon it all the consequences of such neglect.

1 Ca. 166.

IN THE PRECEDING pages the progress of legislation with respect to ship-lights has been detailed, and as an opportunity was taken of introducing into the same statutes clauses applicable to the question of the rule of the road,

I. TRINITY HOUSE REGULATIONS. Oct. 30, 1840.	II. 9 & 10 *V.* c. 100. Jan. 1, 1847.
When steam vessels on different courses must unavoidably or necessarily pass so near, that by continuing their respective courses there would be a risk of coming into collision, each vessel shall put her helm to port, so as always to pass on the larboard side of each other.	§ 9 And be it enacted, that every steam vessel, when meeting or passing any other steam vessel, shall pass, as far as may be safe, on the port side of such other vessel;

it will be sufficient here to remind the reader that of these statutes,

The 9 & 10 Vict., c. 100, came into operation January 1st, 1847, and remained so till December 31st, 1851.

And the 14 & 15 Vict., c. 79, from December 31st, 1851, to May 1st, 1855.

They were succeeded by the 17 & 18 Vict., c. 104, (The Merchant Shipping Act,) which came into operation on May 1st, 1855, and still remains in force.

For the same facility of reference, the clauses relating more immediately to this subject are here printed in parallel columns.

III.
14 & 15 V. c. 79.

Dec. 31, 1851.

§ 27. Whenever any vessel proceeding in one direction, meets a vessel proceeding in another direction, and the master or other person having charge of either such vessel perceives that, if both vessels continue their respective courses, they will pass so near as to involve any risk of a collision, he shall put the helm of his vessel to port, so as to pass on the port side of the other vessel,

due regard being had to the tide and to the position of each vessel,

IV.
17 & 18 V. c. 104
Merchant Shipping Act,

May 1, 1855.

§ 296. Whenever any ship, whether a steam or sailing ship, proceeding in one direction, meets another ship, whether a steam or sailing ship proceeding in another direction, so that if both ships were to continue their respective courses they would pass so near as to involve any risk of a collision, the helms of both ships shall be put to port, so as to pass on the port side of each other. And this rule shall be obeyed by all steam ships and by all sailing ships, whether close hauled or not, unless the circumstances of the case are such as to render a departure from the rule necessary, in order to avoid immediate danger, and subject also to the proviso that due regard shall be had to the dangers of navigation,

I.	II.
TRINITY HOUSE REGULATIONS.	9 & 10 V. c. 100.
A steam vessel passing another in a narrow channel must always leave the vessel she is passing on the larboard side	and every steam vessel navigating any river or narrow channel shall keep as far as is practicable to that side of the fair-way or mid-channel of such river or channel which lies on the starboard side of such vessel, due regard being had to the tide, and to the position of each vessel in such tide. And the master or other person having the charge of any such steam vessel and neglecting to observe these regulations, or either of them, shall, for each and every instance of neglect, forfeit and pay a sum not exceeding fifty pounds.

The remaining clauses of the different statutes relating to this subject are as follows:—

I.	II.	III.
9 & 10 V., c. 100.	14 & 15 V., c. 79.	*Merchant Shipping Act*, 1854, 17 & 18 V., c. 104.
§ 13 And be it enacted, That if any damage to any person or property shall be sustained in consequence of the non-observance, as respects any steam vessel, of the rules contained in the two enactments relative to the passing of steam vessels, "and to the exhibiting of lights," hereinbefore contained, the same shall in all courts of justice be deemed, in the absence of proof to the contrary, to have been occasioned	§ 28. If in any case of a collision between two or more vessels, it appears that such collision was occasioned by the non observance either of the foregoing Rules with respect to the passing of steamers, " or of the Rules to be made as aforesaid by the Lord High Admiral or the Commissioners for executing the office of Lord High Admiral with respect to the exhibition of lights," the Owner of the vessel by	§ 298. If, in any case of collision, it appears to the Court before which the case is tried that such collision was occasioned by the non observance of "any rule for the exhibition of lights or the use of fog-signals, issued in pursuance of the powers hereinbefore contained," or of the foregoing Rule as to the passing of steam and sailing ships, or of the foregoing Rule as to a steam ship keeping to

III
14 & 15 V., c. 79

with respect to the danger of the channel, and as regards sailing vessels to the keeping each vessel under command. And the master of every steam vessel navigating any river or narrow channel shall keep as far as is practicable to that side of the fairway or mid-channel thereof which lies on the starboard side of such vessel. And if the master or other person having charge of any steam vessel neglect to observe these regulations, or either of them, he shall, for every such offence, be liable to a penalty not exceeding fifty pounds,

IV.
17 & 18 V., c. 104.

and as regards sailing ships on the starboard tack close-hauled, to the keeping such ships under command.

§ 297 Every steam ship, when navigating any narrow channel, shall, whenever it is safe and practicable, keep to that side of the fairway or mid-channel which lies on the starboard side of such steam vessel.

I.
9 & 10 V., c. 100.

by the wilful default of the Master or other person having the charge of such steam vessel, and such Master or other person shall be subject in all proceedings, whether civil or criminal, to the legal consequences of such wilful default.

II.
14 & 15 V., c. 79.

which any such Rule has been infringed shall not be entitled to recover any recompense whatsoever for any damage sustained by such vessel in such collision, unless it appear to the Court before which the case is tried that the circumstances of the case were such as to justify a departure from the Rule. And in case any damage to person or property be sustained in consequence of the

III.
17 & 18 V., c. 104.

that side of a narrow channel which lies on the starboard side, the Owner of the ship by which such Rule has been infringed shall not be entitled to recover any recompense whatever for any damages sustained by such ship in such collision, unless it is shown, to the satisfaction of the Court, that the circumstances of the case made a departure from the Rule necessary.

§ 299. In case any damage to person or property arises from the non-observance by

114

I.	II.	III
9 & 10 V, c. 100.	14 & 15 V, c. 79.	17 & 18 V, c. 104.
	non observance of any of the said Rules, the same shall in all courts of justice be deemed, in absence of proof to the contrary, to have been occasioned by the wilful default of the Master or other person having the charge of such vessel, and such Master or other person shall unless it appear to the Court before which the case is tried that the circumstances of the case were such as to justify a departure from the Rule, be subject in all proceedings, whether civil or criminal, to the legal consequences of such default	any ship of any of the said rules, such damage shall be deemed to have been occasioned by the wilful default of the person in charge of the deck of such ship at the time, unless it is shown, to the satisfaction of the Court, that the circumstances of the case made a departure from the Rule necessary.

Jan 9, 1853.

Through some accident the case of the *Adventure* was not stated at length in its proper place, and only a reference made to it; but as it has an important bearing on the construction of the Acts of Parliament, and was the first instance in which it was brought before the Court, it has been judged advisable to supply the omission

In that case a collision had taken place between that vessel and the *William Broderick* on the 4th of October, 1852. These vessels were both proceeding from the N., and had been driven by stress of weather to come to anchor in the Yarmouth Roads. The *William Broderick*, it appeared, at first rode at anchor by her small bower anchor, and hoisted a light in the "pall-bits," about 6 feet above deck. The *Adventure*, it was alleged on her part, was first brought up with her small bower anchor; but as the violence of the gale increased and she began to drive, her best bower anchor was let go; this afterwards parted, and she came with her starboard quarter athwart hawse the *William Broderick,* doing her considerable damage

On the part of the *Adventure*, it was contended that the accident was principally attributable to the neglect of the *William Broderick* in not having a proper light, and hoisting it in the manner required by the Admiralty Regulations

The Court, alluding to the circumstance of this being the first case brought before it since the passing of the Act, proceeded to examine at length its enactments, observing upon the necessity of obedience to the Act, no matter with what severity it might operate; and that these regulations, established under its authority, were as binding as if they had literally formed part of it. that with respect to the place where the vessels were, it was a fairway or roadstead; and therefore this regulation enjoining the use of a light was applicable: that as to the kind of light itself that was required by the Regulations, it was termed in one place a constant bright light, and in another a common bright light, and it was also added that it was left to the parties themselves to furnish themselves with whatever description of lantern they might see fit, provided the conditions in the Regulations were effectually carried out, and in the present case there was no reason to imagine that it was otherwise than a lantern which gave the usual degree of light.

The Court then proceeded to examine the Regulations, and observed that nothing could be more clear, as to the full and entire power of the Lords of the Admiralty to prescribe to British subjects regulations for hoisting lights anywhere and everywhere, as they think fit, and to alter them as they please. It then pointed out what was to be done if the Regulations were not obeyed, viz, that such neglect entailed a penalty of £20, and added, that if nothing more had been said in the Act there would have been an end of the whole matter, and it would not affect a case of collision at all, because, when an Act directs a thing to be done under a penalty, when that penalty has been borne, you cannot carry it into penal consequences not contemplated, or mentioned in the Act of Parliament; but the Act proceeds to add, that if it appear that the collision was occasioned by the non-observance of the Regulations, such neglect shall deprive the party of all right to recover compensation, unless the circumstances of the case were such as to justify a departure from the Act, and, in the construction of this clause, it held that *to occasion* and give cause was one and the same thing; that a collision might be as much occasioned by a vessel being without lights, and another running into it, as by the helm being turned the wrong way, and running into a vessel; and with respect to the exception introduced in the latter part, added that the meaning was this; if you are ordered to exhibit a light at the masthead, you shall obey that order, unless something occurs that shall make it more likely to prevent an accident by exhibiting it in another place, where it is better and more easy to see, that is the common sense meaning of it; and it concluded, that if the Trinity Masters should be of opinion that, in consequence of the light having been exhibited, or rather, having been fastened to the "pall-bits," the *William Broderick* was less visible than if it had been at the masthead, you must find those on board the *William Broderick* to blame; but if they were of opinion that she was equally visible, though it would be a violation of the Act of Parliament, and a penalty would be incurred, yet it would not prevent that vessel recovering in the suit

The Trinity Masters, having expressed their opinion that, under the circumstances, the light was equally efficient on the "pall-bits" as it would have been at the masthead, the Court pronounced in favour of the *William Broderick.*

WITH REFERENCE to the construction of the latter Act (17 & 18 Vict ,c. 104), the following cases will illustrate the interpretation the Court is disposed to put upon it.

1st With reference to the term "meeting or approaching."

In the case of the *Ceres* and *Harmony*, the collision took place on the Thames; the latter vessel, a barge, was on a S E. by S. course, proceeding from London to Feversham, and when off the Nore light, perceived the red light, and afterwards the green light of the other vessel, a steamer; upon observing the red light only, she did not show any light, but did exhibit one immediately the green light became visible

The steamer, her proper course being to the N. of W., was just coming to anchor on account of the darkness of the night, and having starboarded her helm, came to the S. of the mid-channel, when the collision took place.

The Court expressed its opinion that, considering the manner in which these vessels were proceeding, and that only the red light of the steamer was first visible to the *Harmony*, they would have gone clear, if they had kept their courses, and therefore that the Act of Parliament,

June 13, 1857

118

enjoining the showing of a light on approaching another vessel was not applicable in the first instance, although it became so when the green light became visible, and that the *Harmony* having then exhibited a light, was free from blame, that the steamer was in fault for not having proceeded more cautiously by easing and slacking her speed, and therefore condemned her in the damages.

March 6, 1857

In the case of the *Kong Hakon* and the *Mary* the wind was W.S W., both vessels were bound to Newcastle, the *Mary* close-hauled on the port tack, reaching in, and descrying the other vessel a little on the starboard side, at the distance of about a mile, ported her helm.

The *Kong Hakon* close-hauled, standing S., at first kept her course, but afterwards, the danger becoming threatening, ported her helm, but to no purpose, as the vessels came into collision, being both damaged on the port side

The Court expressed its opinion that the *Mary* was to blame for not having ported in time, and condemned her in the damages.

May 22, 1857

In the case of the *Alexandre* and the *Asp*, both these vessels were going free; the *Asp* observed the other vessel at the distance of about half a mile, a point and a half on her starboard bow, and kept her course. The *Alexandre* on the near approach of the *Asp* ported her helm.

The Court expressed its opinion that the *Asp* was to blame for not having ported her helm at all, and the *Alexandre* for not having done so in time, and therefore that both vessels were in fault.

July 15, 1857

In the case of the *Effort* and *Fotine*, the latter vessel was proceeding on the starboard tack, heading S S.E., when observing the *Effort* at the distance of about a mile, she ported and luffed up to the wind. The *Effort*, on the port tack, close-hauled, and on a N. by W. course, on descrying the other vessel, also ported.

The Court observed that these two vessels were meeting each other, and in order to have avoided the collision, ought both to have put their helms to port; and, being of opinion that the *Effort* did not put her helm to port in sufficient time, condemned her in the damages.

In the case of the *Norval* and *Colne* the wind was W.; the *Colne* steering S S E, descried the other vessel about a quarter of a mile, and, as she stated, ported her helm, the *Norval* was steering N N W., and proceeding close-hauled on the port tack, and ported her helm, but the vessels came into collision, the stem and larboard bow of the *Norval* with the starboard bow of the *Colne*.

July 30, 1857.

The Court observed that, although the law required vessels to port when there was danger of a collision, yet the rule was not to be carried to an absurdity, and one vessel is not to cross the course of another, if by keeping their respective courses they might have passed in safety, and being of opinion that the statement of the *Colne* that she had ported her helm could not be reconciled with the manner in which the vessels came into collision, pronounced that vessel to blame, and condemned her in the damages.

In the case of the *Cleopatra*, that vessel, a steamer, came into collision with the *Simlah*, also a steamer, on the 14th August, 1855.

Aug 4, 1856.

The *Cleopatra*, her course being E. ½ N., at the distance of three or four miles, discerned the green and white lights of the other vessel, two points on her starboard bow, and first starboarded her helm, and afterwards, as she alleged, ported it.

The *Simlah*, on a W ½ S course, on perceiving the *Cleopatra*, ported her helm.

The Court, referring to the Act 17 & 18 Vict., c. 104, § 296, observed that the first question was whether these vessels were meeting so as to come within the construction of the statute, adding that in its opinion the meaning of the statute was that whenever two vessels are seen from each other, even in parallel courses, provided they are close to each other, or in any course so that there is reasonable probability of a collision, it is their duty, unless there be some impediment, to obey the statute

In this case the vessels were on directly opposite courses, and the lights of the one were seen only two points on the starboard bow of the other; it therefore fell within the intention of the Act. If one vessel had appeared to be five or six points on the starboard bow of the other, then they would not be considered as meeting each other, the term used in the Act of Parliament, but would be crossing each other, and different considerations would apply. Under all the circumstances, it considered that the *Cleopatra* was solely to blame, and condemned her in the damages.

Vide ante, p. 36

In the case of the *Ericson*, a collision occurred between that vessel, an American vessel, and the barque *Alderman Thompson*

The wind was N W. by N., and the latter vessel was on the port tack, heading E N E., and observed the green light of the steamer broad on her starboard bow, at a distance of about four miles; and on the part of the *Ericson* it was contended that, under these circumstances, she ought, in compliance with the Act of Parliament, to have ported her helm, and have got out of the way

The Court observed that, one vessel being a foreign vessel, the Act of Parliament was not here applicable; had it, however, been, the construction contended for could not be admitted.

If when a green light is seen, and you know the direction in which the steamer is going, and it is upon the starboard side of you, you were to port the helm, the consequences would be that you would bring yourself across the course of the vessel, but the statute directs no such thing, it speaks of there being danger of collision; but as long as the green light is seen broad on the starboard bow, there is no danger of collision. It never was intended that when two vessels see each other at a distance of two miles, supposing that one is on the starboard tack, that that vessel is to begin to change her course, because there is a possibility of a collision. The true construction is that when two vessels are approaching each other, and are within such a distance that there is a strong probability of collision if both keep their courses, in that case both vessels are to port. In this case the helm of the steamer was not ported until the other vessel was less than a quarter of a mile off; and, being of opinion that the *Ericson* was to blame, condemned her in the damages.

In the case of the *James*, that vessel was proceeded against by the *Confucius*, on account of a collision which occurred between them whilst they were both lying to, the *Confucius* on the port tack, her head being from N to N. by E; the *James* on the starboard tack with her head from S.W. by S W by S

The Court below had pronounced them both in fault,—the *Confucius* for not having ported in time, and the *James* for not having done all in her power to avoid the collision,—and directed the damage to be divided between them.

By that decision, as the *James* was a vessel of small value, about £200, and the damage between £6000 and £7000, her whole value would have been absorbed.

Against it an appeal was brought on her part, and the point raised for the first time whether the Act 17 & 18 Vict., c. 104, did not apply to this case, and consequently, whether the *Confucius* not having complied with its regulations respecting porting was not deprived of all right to recover compensation.

The Court of Appeal, the judicial committee of the P C., in giving judgment, observed that these vessels were not proceeding on their several voyages at the time of the collision, but were lying to, and were moving as little as possible: the one with her head toward the N., and the other towards the S.

The object of the Act of Parliament appeared to be to provide a rule by which, in all cases, vessels approaching each other in different directions, so as to involve the risk of a collision, were to adopt a certain course in order to avoid it; then Lordships were of opinion that these vessels were in such circumstances at the time as to bring them within the meaning of the Act, and that the *Confucius*, having neglected to port her helm in compliance with the rule, could not recover in an Admiralty Court even from a vessel also in fault.

Jan. 27, 1857

In the case of the *James Holmes* and the *Viking*, the former vessel was coming up channel close hauled on the port tack and kept her course. The latter vessel was going down channel, *by* the wind, on the starboard tack, and on descrying the *James Holmes*, as she stated, nearly ahead, put her helm to port and luffed up close.

The Court expressed its opinion that as the vessels were approaching end on or nearly end on, the *Viking* did right, in compliance with the Act of Parliament, to port; but if she was four points to leeward, in this case on the starboard bow of the vessel coming up channel, so that to port would be to cross her hawse it could not be within the terms of the Act of Parliament, according to the common sense construction of it, and decided that the *James Holmes* was in fault for not having ported in time.

THE CASE OF AN EXCEPTION to the enactment in favour of vessels "close-hauled" came before the Court.

In the case of the *Inflexible*, that vessel, a steamer in H. M S., came into collision with the *Soubahdar*; the latter vessel was close-hauled on the starboard tack, and just before the collision, descried the steamer at a distance of about a mile, and put her helm to port, the steamer having observed the vessel about seven or eight minutes before the collision, put her helm hard a-port about four minutes previous to the accident

Jan 30, 1856.

The Court, alluding to the exception in the clause, with respect to vessels close-hauled on the starboard tack, observed, that it did not follow that the moment a sailing vessel saw a steamer at a distance, say of three miles, she was to begin to alter her helm, that might be a dangerous thing, supposing she were close-hauled; and accordingly it makes an exception as regards sailing vessels on the starboard tack close-hauled, to the keeping such vessel under command; it does not say that you are to throw yourself into stays, or that you are to lose the command of your vessel, and expressed its opinion that the *Soubahdar* did not port too late, but that the *Inflexible* was solely in fault.

AGAIN, WITH REFERENCE to the "avoiding immediate danger," reference may be made to the following cases:

In the case of the *Sylph* and *Ardina*, the *Ardina*, a Dutch vessel, was proceeding on a voyage from Lisbon to

April 9, 1857.

Vlaardingen, when she perceived the green light of a steamer at a distance of about a mile and a half between three and four points on her starboard bow, and put her helm to starboard, but afterwards, the green light disappearing, and the red light becoming visible at the distance of about half a mile, she ported her helm, and payed off considerably, but to no effect

The steamer was proceeding from London to Dublin, and perceived the other vessel at a distance of about half a mile, about one point on the steamer's port bow, when she ported her helm, but the collision notwithstanding took place, the *Ardina* being struck midship on the port side.

The Court observed that, one being a foreign vessel, the Act of Parliament was not applicable to this case, otherwise it would have been necessary for it to have put the question— whether the circumstances of the case were such that the starboarding of the helm by the *Ardina* was necessary to to avoid immediate danger, adding that, when the green light of a steamer is seen, it is manifest that she is on the starboard side, and if the red light be visible the reverse; and that it accordingly becomes the duty of a vessel to adopt the best means of avoiding a collision in connection with the circumstances, and expressed its opinion that the collision could not have occurred in the manner in which it did, consistently with the statement of the *Sylph*, but only in consequence of her having starboarded her helm, or not having ported it in time or at all, and accordingly condemned her in the damages.

The *Grace Darling* was proceeding up the river Usk, close-hauled on the starboard tack, heading N E., when, perceiving the green and white lights of the *Peru*, a steamer, she starboarded her helm.

The *Peru*, in tow of a tug, was coming down the river, and on descrying the other vessel, the master of the steamer starboarded her helm, and directed the pilot on board the *Peru* to do the same, the tug passed clear, but the *Peru* and the *Grace Darling* came into collision

The Court observed that, under the circumstances of the green light being only visible, the *Grace Darling* could only avoid the collision by starboarding her helm, that the other vessel was to blame, that the fault was partly that of the master of the steamer and pilot, and that the *Peru* appeared to be more than ordinarily incapable of being steered, that the owners of the brig were responsible for such condition of the vessel, and also for the acts of the tug, and therefore condemned them in the damages.

In the case of the *Joseph Somes* and the *Glanmire*, the *Glanmire*, as she stated, close-hauled on the starboard tack, on perceiving the other vessel, at first ported her helm, but on the collision being imminent, starboarded it, to avoid immediate danger. the *Joseph Somes* with the wind free ported her helm, but not immediately.

The Court expressed its opinion that the case fell within the exception mentioned in the Act of Parliament of avoiding immediate danger, and that the *Glanmire* was justified in what she did, but that the *Joseph Somes* was in fault in having delayed to port in due time.

AND WITH REFERENCE to a vessel being "under com-"mand,"

In the case of the *Berbice* and *Effort* these vessels came into collision in the Irish channel. The wind was blowing from the E The former vessel, on a voyage from Liverpool, sailing free, perceived the other vessel at a distance of a quarter of a mile, and ported her helm The *Effort* close-hauled on the starboard tack, her head being to the N E., kept her course.

The Court expressed its opinion that the case of the *Effort* fell within the exception of the Act of Parliament, and that in order to keep the vessel under command she was justified in not putting her helm more to port than she did, and that the *Berbice* was to blame for not having ported her helm, as she might have done, in due time

WITH REFERENCE to the navigation of "narrow channels," the opinion of the Court has been expressed in the following cases

May 5, 1856
Vide ante, p 58.

In the case of the *Neptune*, the collision occurred between that vessel, a steamer, and the *Unity* sloop in the river Tyne.

The Court referring to the § 297 of the 17 & 18 Vict c. 104, respecting the navigation by steamers in narrow channels, and the expression of "safe and practicable" used in it, expressed its opinion that where there is no local impediment of any kind, no difficulty arising from the peculiar formation of the channel itself, no storm or wind, or anything of that kind occurring, then the obligation continues to keep to the starboard side, and no consideration of convenience, no opportunity of accelerating the speed, can justify a disobedience of the statute; nor could any local custom as to the navigation of a particular channel be allowed to supersede the Act, and expressed its opinion that the *Neptune* was to blame for not porting her helm in time, but as the *Unity* was also in fault in other respects, neither party could recover

Jan 27, 1857

In the case of the *Silloth* and *Admiral Boxer*, the collision took place between these vessels in the river Mersey;

the former, a steamer on a voyage from Liverpool, on perceiving the other vessel, put her helm to port. The *Admiral Boxer*, returning to Liverpool, perceiving the green light of the steamer, put her helm to starboard, and afterwards on the red one being visible, put it to port.

On the part of the *Admiral Boxer*, it was pleaded and contended that the steamer, in violation of the § 297, stood over to the wrong side of the channel, and that she had not ported in time, and that the former vessel was justified in the steps she took in consequence of the appearance of the lights on board the steamer.

The Court, however, was of opinion that the *Silloth* was not in fault, but that the *Admiral Boxer* was to blame, for having starboarded her helm, but that she was exonerated from responsibility under the Pilot Act.

THE OPINION OF THE COURT respecting the construction to be put upon the term "occasioned," has been expressed in several cases which had occurred under the former Act, and many of them have been detailed at length in the former part of this work. Under the present Act the following cases may also be referred to.

In the case of the *Loftus* and the *James and Ann*, the latter vessel was going up the Bristol Channel, her course N.E. by N., on perceiving the *Loftus* at the distance of about a mile, she put her helm to port, bringing the *Loftus* broad under her lee, the helm being afterwards starboarded to ease the blow, but did not show a light. The *Loftus* pleaded that on account of the darkness of the night she had not seen the other vessel till she was within one-eighth of a mile, and that she then ported her helm. The Court observed that the *James and Ann* was clearly bound by

128

the Act and Admiralty Regulations to have shown a light, and the question therefore was, whether the collision was owing to her neglect in not having done so, but expressed its opinion that such was not the case, but that the *Loftus* was in fault in not having ported in time.

Nov. 13, 1856.

In the case of the *Shannon* and *Lady Anne*, the latter vessel proceeded against the former on account of a collision which had occurred between them. the *Shannon*, a steamer, was proceeding on a course N.E. by N, and on descrying the other vessel immediately put her helm to port, but did not stop her engines, the *Lady Anne* was close-hauled on the starboard tack, on S.W by S course, and first perceived the *green* light of the steamer, afterwards the *red* light became visible, but she kept on her course.

The Court observed, that although primâ facie a vessel, on perceiving the green light of a steamer approaching, would incur great risk of running into her by porting, and therefore the non-observance of the Act of Parliament would be justifiable, in this case, however, it was of opinion that the *Lady Anne* was to blame, for not having ported her helm when the red light became visible, and that such neglect was the occasion of the accident; she could not therefore recover the damages against the other vessel, but as it was also of opinion that the steamer was in fault, for not having stopped her engines, it dismissed the suit without costs.

IN OTHER CASES to which the Act is not applicable, as also in those of foreign vessels, the general maritime law still remains in force.

March 25, 1857.

In the case of the *Undine* and *Auspicious*, the night was dark, with heavy rain at times. The *Auspicious* was close-hauled on the port tack, and, descrying the light of the steamer three points on her weather bow, kept her course. The *Undine*, a steamer, wind free, observed the light of the other vessel about three points and a half on her starboard bow, and starboarded her helm.

The Court expressed its opinion that the *Undine* was alone to blame, and condemned her in the damages.

In the case of the *Linda Flor* and the *Haarburg*, the former vessel, on a voyage from Hamburg to Oporto, alleging the darkness of the night as a reason for not having seen the other vessel till just before the collision, had done nothing to avoid it. The latter vessel on a voyage from Hamburg to Bordeaux, perceiving the *Linda Flor* four or five points on her port bow, at the distance of about half a mile, kept close to the wind, and, finding the collision inevitable, put her helm hard to port.

The Court expressed its opinion that the *Haarburg* had done everything in her power; but that the *Linda Flor* had not kept a good look out, and being on the port tack, was solely to blame for the collision.

In the case of the *Activ*, a foreign vessel, and the *Alert*, the *Alert* was proceeding to the S, close-hauled on the starboard tack, and on observing the other vessel, at the distance of about a mile, showed a light over the starboard side, and kept her course. The *Activ* was sailing behind the other vessel with the wind free, when she observed the other vessel three points on her port bow, three or four hundred yards distant, and ported her helm, but to no purpose.

The Court having observed that the *Activ*, sailing free, was bound to get out of the way of another vessel close-hauled, expressed its opinion that she was in fault, and condemned her in the damages.

April 3, 1857

Vide ante, p 73

Jan 30, 1857.

In the case of the *Rival* and the *Express*, the latter had brought up in the Yarmouth Roads about noon of the 22nd August, 1856, and the former, about seven o'clock of the same day, anchored in her vicinity, when a collision took place between them.

The Court expressed its opinion that the *Rival* had given the other vessel foul berth, and condemned her in the damages.

APPENDIX.

FOREIGN ORDINANCES

AMERICA
DENMARK
FRANCE
HOLLAND.
MECKLENBURGH

NORWAY.
PRUSSIA
RUSSIA
SWEDEN.

FOREIGN ORDINANCES.

FRANCE.

Moniteur Universel, Mercredi, 18 Août, 1852

République Française

Rapport au Prince Président de la République Française.

Monseigneur,

Les navigateurs de toutes les nations se sont toujours préoccupés des nombreux sinistres résultant des abordages des navires entr'eux, et ont constamment recherché des moyens efficaces pour les prévenir

Le développement progressif de la marine à vapeur avoit surtout appelé l'attention générale sur la nécessité de certaines dispositions propres à écarter les dangers de la navigation pendant la nuit. Un système uniforme d'éclairage pour tous les bâtimens à vapeur fut adopté par plusieurs puissances maritimes, à l'imitation de la France et de l'Angleterre, qui dès l'année 1848, avaient admis, d'un commun accord, un règlement sur cet objet important.

Sans doute la généralisation d'une semblable mesure, si utile à bord de tous les navires à vapeur, était déjà un véritable progrès, mais ce système d'éclairage ne s'applique qu'à la marine à vapeur, et les navires à voiles restent exposés aux mêmes dangers pendant leur navigation de nuit, notamment ceux qui fréquentent les côtes ou des parties de mer resserrés.

Afin de combler une telle lacune, et d'astreindre tous les marins à l'exécution rigoureuse des dispositions relatives aux feux que les navires de l'état et du commerce doivent porter pendant la nuit, j'ai l'honneur de soumettre à votre approbation le projet de décret ci-joint

Je suis, avec le plus profond respect,

Monseigneur,

Votre très humble et très dévoué serviteur,

Le Ministre Secrétaire d'État, de la Marine, et des Colonies

THEODORE DUCOS.

LOUIS NAPOLÉON,
Président de la République Française.

LOUIS NAPOLEON,

Président de la République Française

Sur le Rapport de notre Ministre Secretaire d'Etat, de la Marine, et des Colonies

Décrète

Art 1er A l'avenir, tous les navires à vapeur et à voiles de l'Etat porteront, depuis le coucher du soleil jusqu'à son lever, des feux dont la couleur et la disposition sont indiquées ci après pour chaque espèce de bâtiment.

Art. 2 Les navires à vapeur, à roues, ou à hélice, lorsqu'ils feront route, soit au large, soit près des côtes, soit dans l'interieur des *ports*, des *rades*, des *baies*, et des *rivieres*, parteront

1° Un feu blanc en tête du mât de misaine,

2° Un feu vert à tribord,

3° Un feu rouge à babord, et, lorsqu'ils seront à l'ancre, un feu blanc ordinaire en tête du mât de misaine.

Le feu de tête du mât devra être visible à une distance d'au moins cinque milles, par une nuit claire, et le fanal sera construit de telle sorte que sa lumière soit uniforme et non interrompue dans un arc de vingt rumbs de vent (223°), c'est-à-dire, depuis le cap du bâtiment jusqu'à deux quarts en arrière du travers de chaque bord

Les feux de couleur devront être visible d'une distance d'au moins deux milles, par une nuit claire, et les fanaux construits de maniere à ce que la lumière embrasse, sans interruption ni variation d'éclat, un arc de l'horizon de dix quarts (112° 30'), c'est-à-dire, depuis le cap du navire jusqu'à deux quarts de l'arrière du travers du bord où ils sont placés.

Les fanaux de côté seront construits de telle sorte qu'on ne puisse apercevoir leur lumière a travers le bâtiment

Le fanal employé au mouillage devra donner une bonne lumière tout autour de l'horizon.

Art. 3 Les bâtiments à voiles de l'Etat, marchant à la voile, ou à la remorque, ou à la touée, ou s'approchant d'un autre navire, ou en étant approchés, seront tenus de porter, entre le coucher et le lever du soleil, une lumière brillante placée de façon à être aperçue par tout autre navire, te en temps suffisant pour éviter un abordage

Les navires à voiles de l'Etat etant à l'ancre, sur une rade, seront auss tenus de hisser en tête du mât, entre le coucher et le lever du soleil, une feu clair et continu, excepté dans des ports où des règlemens particuliers prescriraient d'autres feux de position

Toutefois, lorsque les bâtimens de guerre mouillés sur une rade, auron besoin de signaler leur position d'une manière plus complète, ou suivan l'ordre de service établi dans une division navale à laquelle ils appartien draient, ces bâtimens se conformeront aux instructions générales de la tactique navale (Art 51, pages 309, 310)

Le fanal à l'usage des navires à voiles, quand ils seront à l'ancre, devra être installé de façon à éclairer tous les points de l'horizon.

Art. 4 Tout navire de commerce à voile et à vapeur sera tenu de se conformer rigoureusement aux dispositions applicables aux navires à voiles et à vapeur de l'Etat, excepté en ce qui concerne les feux de position prescrits par la tactique navale.

Art. 5. Tous les règlemens antérieurs relatifs aux feux que doivent porter les navires à vapeur sont et demeurent abrogés

Art. 6 Des instructions spéciales détermineront l'emploi des feux dont il est fait mention dans les articles précédents

Art. 7. Le Ministre Secretaire d'Etat, de la Marine, et des Colonies, est chargé de l'execution du present décret

Fait au Palais de Ste Cloud, le 17 Août, 1852
LOUIS NAPOLEON.

Par le Prince President,
Le Ministre Secretaire d'Etat, de la Marine, et des Colonies,
THEODORE DUCOS

PREVIOUS TO THIS DECREE, a similar one, but confined to steam vessels, had been made, bearing date the 14th October, 1848, in connection with which a set of diagrams were drawn up to illustrate its proposed working These were composed in the following form.

INSTRUCTION TRANSMISE PAR LE GOUVERNEMENT AUX CHAMBRES DE COMMERCE, A L'ÉPOQUE DU DECRET DU 14 OCTOBRE, 1848

Les Gouvernements de France et d'Angleterre, dans le but d'éviter, pendant la nuit, la rencontre en mer des navires à vapeur et de prevenir les sinistres, qui sont la consequence des abordages, ont d'un commun accord, adopté le système suivant de tactique et d'eclairage A l'avenir, tous les bâtimens à vapeur anglais et français, porteront depuis le coucher du soleil jusqu'à son lever, des feux dont la disposition est indiquée ci après.

Lorsqu'ils feront route
    1° Un feu blanc en tête du mât de misaine ;
    2° Un feu vert à tribord ;
    3° Un feu rouge à babord
Lorsqu'ils seront au mouillage
    Un feu blanc ordinaire
Ils se conformeront aux conditions suivantes savoir,

1. Le feu de tête de mât devra être visible à une distance d'au moins cinq milles par une nuit claire, et le fanal sera construit de telle sorte que la lumière soit uniforme et non interrompue dans un arc de vingt rumbs de

vent (223°), c'est-à-dire, depuis le cap du bâtiment jusqu'à deux quarts en arrière du travers de chaque bord

2 Les feux de couleur devront être visibles d'au moins deux milles par une nuit claire, et les fanaux construits de manière à ce que la lumière embrasse, sans interruption ni variations d'éclat, un arc de l'horizon de dix quarts (112° 30'), c'est-à-dire, depuis le cap du navire jusqu'à deux quarts de l'arrière du travers du bord où ils sont placés

3 Les feux de côté seront garnis en dedans d'écrans ayant au moins trois pieds de longueur, afin qu'on ne puisse les apercevoir à travers le bâtiment ils seront appliqués longitudinalement en avant et en arrière de la face intérieure des fanaux latéraux

4 Le fanal employé au mouillage sera construit de manière à donner une bonne lumière tout au tour de l'horizon

FIGURES.

Les figures suivantes ont pour but de préciser l'usage des feux qui viennent d'être indiquées

Première Position
(See diagram, page 25)

Dans cette position, le vapeur A ne voit que le feu rouge du vapeur B, quelle que soit celle des trois directions du plan que B suive, attendu que le feu vert de ce dernier reste toujours masqué A est donc bien sûr que B lui présente le côté de bâbord, et qu'il gouverne de manière à lui couper la route de tribord à bâbord , A peut donc en toute confiance (s'il fait assez noir pour qu'il redoute un abordage) venir sur tribord.

Il ne court aucun risque de rencontrer B. D'un autre côté, B, dans ses trois positions, voit le feu rouge, le feu vert et le feu de tête de A, il les voit sous forme de triangle, et sait par là que A court droit sur lui, B manœuvre en consequence

Il est inutile de remarquer que les feux de tête de mât seront visibles de part et d'autre jusqu'à ce que le travers de chacun des vapeurs ait été dépassé de deux quarts sur l'arrière

Deuxième Position
(See diagram, page 26)

A ne voit que le feu vert de B, ce qui lui indique clairement que B lui coupe la route de bâbord à tribord.

B voit au contraire les trois feu de A, et en conclut qu'un vapeur court opont sur lui

On the whole these directions correspond almost exactly to the English, except as opposite

Troisieme Position.

(See diagram, page 26.)

A et B voient respectivement leurs feux rouges, les feux vert sont masqués par les écrans, il est évident que les navires passeront à babord l'un de l'autre.

Quatrieme Position

(See diagram, page 27)

A et B voient respectivement leurs feux verts, les feux rouges sont masqué par les écrans, les deux navires passeront à tribord l'un de l'autre

Cinquieme Position.[1]

Ce cas demande de l'attention. Le feu rouge qui est aperçu par A et le feu vert par B annoncent aux vapeurs qu'ils s'approchent obliquement l'un de l'autre. A viendra sur tribord, conformement à la règle posée par le cas suivant.

Nota.—La manœuvre indiquée par le tacticien anglais, quoique assez généralement suivie ou au moins généralement recommandée, pourrait, dans certains cas, être fort dangereuse Elle a pour but constant de faire passer le navire B devant A, qui seul doit manœuvrer pour éviter l'abordage Le seul moyen d'obvier au danger qui pourroit résulter de cette manœuvre, sera de prescrire que A, en venant sur tribord, doit stopper et ne mettre en route que lorsque B l'aura dépassé de l'avant.

Si le navire A ne se conformait pas à cette dernière prescription il serait responsable des avaries résultant d un abordage

Sixieme Position.

(See diagram, page 27)

Ici chacun des deux vapeurs aperçoit les deux feux de couleur de l'autre, ce fait indique qu'ils courent droit l'un sur l'autre Dans ce cas, ce devrait être une règle absolue que tous les deux viendraient sur tribord, cette règle est déjà presque généralement adoptée, mais il serait beaucoup plus sûr qu'elle fût rendue obligatoire, car il est évident que sans une règle semblable bien comprise et fidèlement suivie, il est impossible de préserver d'un abordage deux vapeurs qui se trouveront dans la position indiquée par la figure.

[1] In this case the two vessels are placed obliquely to one another, B being on A's starboard

La manière d'établir les feux de couleur doit être l'objet d'une attention particulière. Il faut que chacun d'eux soit muni intérieurement d'un écran de bois ou de toile, afin qu'ils ne puissent être vus à la fois que d'une seule direction, celle du cap du navire même.

Ceci est fort important, car sans les écrans aucune combinaison des feux de côté ne saurait donner une idée précise de la route suivi par le navire.

L'évidence de ce fait, résulte de l'inspection des figures qui précèdent. Dans tous les cas, l'inspection des feux indique à l'instant la route relative que suivent les deux vapeurs, c'est à-dire que chacun d'eux sait de suite si l'autre court droit sur lui, ou bien s'il lui coupe la route de tribord à barbord, ou de babord à tribord.

Il n'en faut pas d'avantage pour que les vapeurs s'évitent par la nuit la plus noire, aussi facilement qu'en plein jour, et pour qu'on ne voie plus le retour des déplorables accidents de ce genre, qui sont arrivés.

NOTE.—For further information respecting the French law in cases of collision, see "SIBILLE sur l'Abordage."

AMERICA.

The rules of Navigation of this country are founded on the generally known usage of Maritime nations, and are the same as those contained in the regulations of the Trinity House.

The only legislative enactments appear to be the Act of Congress of the 7th July, 1838,[1] requiring steamers to carry one or more lights after sunset, and those of several of the States to the same effect, but which are very imperfect, from the want of sufficient detail as to the description and position of the lanterns.

DENMARK.
NOTICE.
(TRANSLATION.)

Regulations to be observed by Commanders of Steamers and Sailing Vessels meeting each other.

In furtherance of His Majesty's most gracious commands, the following Rules, calculated to prevent collision, and the danger which attends it, are

[1] *Osprey*, S G., Ju 11, 1852

published for the guidance of the Captains of Steamers and Sailing Vessels under the Danish Flag

1. If two steamers coming in opposite directions should, by keeping their respective courses, approach each other so closely that a collision is to be apprehended, the Commanders of both vessels must in time bear away to the starboard of each other, so that they pass each other on the larboard side; and they therefore must both put the helm a-port.

   Of course when ships, from not having adopted this rule in time, shall have come so near to each other that the danger of collision is imminent, the experience of the Masters must determine if the position of the vessels at the time requires a deviation from this rule, by backing, or putting the helm the opposite way, but each party is answerable for his conduct on such occasions

2. Steam vessels must always make way for sailing vessels on a wind, as they are to be considered as ships going before the wind

3. If a sailing vessel going before the wind, or free, and a steamer steering an opposite course, approach each other, they must, according to the rule, both bear away to the starboard of each other in time, and, consequently, each put her helm a port.

4. Every steamer at night, whether the weather be clear or not, must exhibit a lantern, with a good light, on the fore part of each of the paddle-boxes, and also at the top of the foremast.

5. When a sailing vessel descries a steamer at night, and expects that her course will bring them so near together that a collision may be feared, then the sailing vessel shall show a lantern until the steamer has passed.

6. If two steamers meet where the river in one or more places is so narrow that they cannot without delay easily pass each other without the fear of coming in contact, then that vessel which through the narrowest part of the passage has to steer a course lying E by S to W inclusive, or if it be on a river, that ship which is going against the stream,—shall remain outside the narrows, or return back from thence, until the other vessel has passed

7. If the arrival in such a river occurs in the dark, or during thick weather, so that the narrow channel cannot be surveyed, the steamer before she enters, whatever course she takes, must announce her arrival by blue light, or by a gun

8. If the Commander of a steamer continues his course in thick weather, he is bound to diminish his speed, ring the ship's bell, and keep a sharp look out, in order to prevent collision

Royal Board of Trade and Customs, Copenhagen,
  9th August, 1844
Danish General Consulate London,
  28th August, 1844

HOLLAND.

Nachtsignale für Seeschiffe. *
1853

AMSTERDAM, *im April.*

Einem Königlichen Beschlosz vom 17 Marz, zufolge mussen alle Segelschifle gleichviel ob unter Segel oder im Schlepptau befindlich, von Sonnen untergang bis Sonnen-aufgang bei Annaherung eines audem Schiffes ein Solches licht zeigen, dasz es von dem etwa sich nahernden Schiffe aus zeitig genug gesehen werden kann um eine kollision zu vermeiden.

Alle auf Rheden und Stromen vor anker liegenden Segelschiffe mussen wohrend ders Nacht ebenfalls ein helles Licht zeigen, und zwar vom Grosztop mit Ausnahme an solchen Orten, wo anderweitige hafensreglements existiren und mussen die Laternen welche die zu Anker liegenden Schiffe gebrauchen, so beschaffen sein, dass das Licht von allen Seiten gesehen werden Kann Die obigen Bestimmungen sind bekanntlich nach Vorgang der Englischen Admiralitat bereits von verschiedenen anderen Nationen eingefuhrt.

Die fur die aus und nach see passirenden See Dampschifle geltenden Bestimmungen von 9 Dezember, 1845, und 29 Januar, 1850, in Betreff der wahrend der Nacht auch von ihnen und zwar zur Erkennung ihres Kurses, zu fuhrenden Signollaternen bleiben in kraft

* *Naut Gesellsch zu Stettin*, 1854.

Night Signals for Sea-going Ships.
1853

AMSTERDAM, *April*

In conformity with a royal decree of the 17th March, all sailing vessels, whether under sail or being towed, are required from sunset to sunrise, on the approach of another vessel, to show such a light as may be seen by the vessel thus approaching in sufficient time to avoid a collision

All sailing vessels lying at anchor in roadsteads or streams are reuired during the night to show in the same manner a clear light, and that at the top of the mast, excepting in those places in which different Harbour Regulations are in existence. And the lanterns which ships lying at anchor make use of are required to be so arranged that the light may be seen from all sides. The above Regulations have been already, as it is well known, adopted after the example of the English Admiralty by other different nations.

The Regulations of the 9th December, 1845, and 29th January, 1850, respecting signal-lanterns, which sea steamers going out or coming in must carry during the night, for the purpose of showing their course remain in force.

MECKLENBERG SCHWERIN.

Verordnung in Betreff der Nacht signals bei Seeschiffen
1853

SCHWERIN, *den 26 Dezember*

Eine grossherzogliche Verordnung vom 22 d verfugt daruber, in Uebereinstimmung mit den Vorschriften anderer seefahrenden Nationen, folgendes

§ 1 Segelschiffe sollen so wohl auf der Fahrt, als auch, wenn sie an Stellen ankern, wo eine Begegnung mit andern, Fahrzeugen statt finden kann, von Sonnenuntergang bis Sonnen aufgang ein helles weisses Licht fuhren. Unter Segel, ist das Licht an einer Stelle des Schiffes anzubringen, wo es den Umstanden nach am besten von sich nahernden Schiffen erkannt werden kann Von Anker ist das Licht an der Mastspitze auzubringen, es muss so eingerichtet sein, dass es einen hellen klaren Schein nach allen Seiten verbreitet

§ II Dampfschiffe mit Radern oder Schranben fuhren.

(a) So lange Sie auf der Fahrt sind ein helles weisses Licht an der vordersten Mastspitze, ein grünes Licht an der Steuerbordseite, ein rothes auf der Backbordseite, das weisse Licht muss so eingerichtet sein, dass es einen gleichmassigen, ununterbrochenen Schein uber einen Bogen von 20 Compass strichen verbreitet und in dunkeln Nachten bei klarer Luft auf 5 Seemeilen entfernung sichtbar ist, das grune, wie das rothe Licht

Regulations respecting Night Signa for Sea going Vessels
1853.

SCHWERIN, *December 26*

An ordonnance of the Grand Duke relating to night signals, and in conformity with the Regulations of other maritime nations, which bears date the 22nd of this month, directs as follows

§ 1 Sailing vessels shall, as well on their voyage, as when they are at anchor in places where a collision with other vessels might take place, from sunset to sunrise, carry a clear white light, when under sail, the light is to be placed in some part of the ship where, according to circumstances, it can best be perceived by vessels approaching When at anchor, the light is to be placed at the top of the mast It must be so placed that it may show a clear distinct light on all sides.

§ II Steam vessels with paddles or screws shall carry—

(a) As long as they are on their voyage a clear white light at the top of the foremast, a green light on the starboard, and a red one on the larboard side The white light must be so arranged that it may show a uniform unbroken light over an arc of 20 points of the compass, and in a dark night with a clear atmosphere may be visible to the distance of 5 sea miles The green light as well as the red light must be so arranged that it

mussen, eingerichtet sein dass sie einen gleichmassigen ununterbrochenen Schein uber einen Bogen von 10 Kompassstrichen seitwarts verbreiten und in dunkeln Nachten bei klarer Luft auf 2 Seemeilen Entfernung sichtbar sind. Die farbigen Lanternen sind an der Seite des Schiffsdecks mit mindestens 3 Foss hochen Schirmen zu versehen, so dass das Licht der einen Seite nicht auf der andern Seite gesehen werden kann.

(b) Vor Ankerliegend gleich den Segelschiffen an der Mastspitze ein helles, nach allen Seiten sichtbares weisses Licht.

§ 2. Fur die Beobachtung diese Vorschriften ist der Schifer, der das Schiff fuhrt, verantworlich, und eventuell fur die Folgen der Unterlassung verhaftet.

may show a uniform unbroken light over an arc of 10 points of the compass sidewards, and in a dark night with a clear atmosphere may be visible to the distance of 2 sea miles. The coloured lanterns placed on the side of the deck of the ship are to be provided with screens of at least 3 feet in height, so that the light on one side may not be seen on the other.

(b). When lying at anchor, they are in the same manner as sailing vessels to carry at the top of the mast a clear white light visible on all sides.

§ 2. For the observance of these Regulations the master who has charge of the vessel is answerable and is held liable to the consequences of the neglect of them.

NORWAY

See SWEDEN.

PRUSSIA.

DIE NACHTSIGNALE FUR SEGEL UND DAMPFFSCHIFFE

Der Minister fur Handel, &c., macht unterm 9 Juli bekannt, dasz, in Uebereinstimmung mit dengenigen Vorschriften, welche bereits von andern Regierungen uber diesen Gegenstand erlassen sind, folgende Bestimmungen erlassen sind, nach welchen sich alle Preus

NIGHTSIGNALS FOR SAILING VESSELS AND STEAMERS

The Minister for Commerce, &c., makes known, under date of the 9th July, that in conformity with those rules, which have already been issued by other governments on this subject, the following regulations are established, and according to them the masters of

sischen schiffer zu richten haben, die mit ihren Fahrzeugen das offene Meer, und die zwischen dem offenen Meer und den Hafenstadten Danzig, Stettin, Wolgast, Greifswold, Stralsund, und Barth belegenen, Binnengewasser, so wie das frische und curische Haff befahren, oder darauf vor anker gehen—insofern nicht für den ort, an welchen sie sich befinden, abweichende gesetzliche order polizeiliche Bestimmungen bestehen

1 Segelschiffe und segelfahrzeuge fuhren uberall, wo eine Begegnung mit andern Fahrzeugen statt finden kann, von sonnen untergang bis sonnen aufgang ein *helles weiszes licht*

Unter segel ist das licht an derjenigen stelle anzubringen, wo es am besten von andern sich naherrnden schiffen erkannt werden kann

Vor anker ist das licht an der mastspisze zu befestigen, und musz so eingerichtet sein, dasz es einen hellen klaren schein nach aller seiten des horizonts verbreitet

2 Dampffschiffe mit radern oder schrauben fuhren

1 So lange sie in der fahrt sind,

    Ein helles weiszes licht an der vordersten mastspitz

    Ein grünes licht auf der steuerbordseite.

    Ein rothes licht auf der backbordseite.

(a) Das weisze licht am vordern mast musz so eingerichtet sein, dasz es einen gleichmaszigen ungebrochenen schein uber einen bogen von 20 kompaszstrichen,—mithin vom bugspriet zwei striche hinter den segelbalken an jeder seite des schiff

all Prussian vessels who navigate with their vessels the open sea, or frequent the towns of Danzic, Stettin, Wolgast, Greisswald, Stralsund, and Barth, and the inland waters, or anchor therein, provided that in the place where they may be no different legal or police regulations are established.

1. Sailing vessels and craft are to carry, everywhere where a collision with another vessel can occur, from sunset to sunrise, a clear white light.

When under sail the light is to be placed in that situation where it can best be seen by another vessel approaching it.

When at anchor the light is to be fastened at the top of the mast, and to be so arranged that it may exhibit a clear light to all sides of the horizon.

2 Steamers with paddles or screws are to carry—

1. So long as they are on their voyage

    A clear white light on the top of the foremost mast

    A green light on the starboard side.

    A red light on the port side.

(a) The white light on the foremost mast must be so placed that it may show a uniform and unbroken light over an arc of 20 points of the compass from the head to 2 points abaft the beam on either side In steam vessels which frequent the

verbreitet. Bei dampfschiffen, welche das offene meer befahren, musz diese leuchte in dunklen nachten bei klaren luft auf 5 seemeilen entfernung sichtbar sein.

(b) Das grüne licht auf der steuerbordseite und das rothe licht auf der backbordseite, müssen so eingerichtet sein, dasz sie einen gleichmassigen ungebrochenen schein über einen bogen von 10 kompaszstrichen, vom bugspriet bis auf zwei kompaszstriche hinter dem segelbalken, seitwärts verbreiten. Bei dampfschiffen, welche das offene meer befahren müssen diese beiden leuchten in dunklen nachten bei klarer luft auf 2 seemeilen entfernung sicht bar sein.

(c) Die farbigen seitenlaternen sind an der seite des schiffsdecks mit mindestens 3 fusz hohen schirmen zu versehen, so dasz das licht der einen seite nicht nach der andern seite gesehen werden kann.

2. Dampfschiffe vor anker führen gleich den segelschiffen auf der mastspitze ein helles nach allen seiten des horizonts sichtbares weiszes licht.

open sea these must, in a dark night with a clear atmosphere, be visible to the distance of 5 sea miles.

(b) The green light on the starboard side, and the red light on the port side must be so disposed that they may exhibit a uniform unbroken light over an arc of 10 points of the compass, from right ahead to 2 points abaft the beam sideways. In steamers which frequent the open sea both these lights must be visible, in a dark night with a clear atmosphere, to the distance of 2 sea miles.

(c) The coloured side lanterns are on the side of the deck to be provided with screens at least 3 feet high, so that the lights on one side may not be seen on the other.

2. Steamers when at anchor are, in the same manner as sailing vessels, to carry at the top of the mast a clear white light visible on all sides of the horizon.

RUSSIA.

Nachtsignale für Seeschiffe
1853

St Petersburg, den 20 April.

Unsere Blätter enthalten ein Reglement vom 13 Marz, wodurch die (nach Vorgang der Englischen Admiralität) bereits, wie bekannt, von mehreren anderen Nationen einge-

Night Signals for Sea-going Vessels
1853

St Petersburg, April 20.

Our pages contain an ordonnance of the 13th March, according to which the Regulations respecting the use of signal lanterns for the purpose of avoiding collision—which,

führten Bestimmungen über den Gebrauch von Signal-laternen zur Vermeidung von Zusammenstossen, nunmehr auch russischer seits für Kriegs-und Post-Schiffe, so wie für die Fahrzeuge des St. Petersburgischens Jacht-Clubbs und für Kauffartheischiffe eingeführt werden

after the example of the English Admiralty, have, as is well known, been already adopted by many other nations—are now also adopted on the part of Russia for ships of war, and those employed in the service of the post, as also for the vessels of the St. Petersburg Yacht Club, and for merchant vessels.

Pravila.

Dlia upotraiblay nia raznotzvetnigh ognaye na Voennigh Potchtovigh Spb. Yacht-Clooba i Koopaytcheskigh Sovdagh vo iz biayshaniay stolknovenni.

Directions

For the use of the different lights on board of vessels of war, post-office packets, vessels of the St. Petersburgh Yacht Club, and merchant vessels, so as to prevent collision.

1 *Dlia Paroghodnigh Soodoff*

Vsceam Paroghodnim soodam ot zaghoshdiaynia do vosghoda solntza vo vsceagh moriagh zalivagh, proli vagh booghtagh gavanyiagh portagh i naykagh i vi kakkigh bi to i beelo obstoyiattelstvagh diayrshat ogni vi slay dooyooshtchem poriadkiay.

1 *For Steam Vessels*

On board of all steam vessels, from sunset to sunrise, in all seas, gulfs, straits, bays, inlets, ports, and rivers, at whatsoever distance the vessels may be, the light is to be shown in the following manner

A *Na ghodoo.*

Yarki ogon vi fonarriay biaylafvo tzvetta na toppiay fok matchtee.

Zaylayni ogon na pravom kos jooghay

Krazni ogon na hayvom kos jooghay

1. Ogon na toppiay fok-matchtee dolshain bi,at vidien vi temnooyoo notch pri tchistoi atmosfayriay na raztoyanniee po krainyay myayray piyattee mil i fonar slaydooyett oostroit takkim obrazzom tchetto bee brosal rofineo i may prayreefniee sviyet po doogay horizontavi dvadzat

A *If in motion.*

A bright light in a lantern of a white colour on the top of the foremast

A green light on the starboard side.

A red light on the port side

1. The lights at the top of the foremast must be visible in a dark night with a clear atmosphere at a distance of at least 5 miles, and the lantern is to be so constructed as to throw a straight and uninterrupted light over an arc of the horizon of 20 points of the compass, i e , for 10

roomboff kompasaa t.e po diaysiati roomboff po kashdooyoo storonoo soodna immenno ot nossa do dvoogh roomboff pozadi traversa si kashdoi storonoo

2 Zaylaini ogon na pravom koshooghay dolshayn biat vidien vi tem nooyoo notch pri tchistoi atmosfayriay po kricenniay miayray na rastoyani dvoogh mil a fonar mayob ghodimo oostroit takkeem obrazom tchettobee brosal roffnee i nayprayreeffnee sviyet po doogay horizonta vi diaysiat roomboft kompassa a immenno ot nossa do dvoodh room boff pozadee traversa si pravoi storonee.

3 Krasni ogon na hayvom koshooghiay shiyay dooath raspoleesheet tak tchtobee brosal swiayt na takkeay shay rastoyanniay si hayvoi storonee

4 Bokoveeay fonar dolshnee beat snabshaynee shtcheetammee so vnoot. renniay storonee po kricniay miayray vi tri foota dlinayoo dlia tovo tchtobee sviaytigh mog biat vidien niay eenatchay kak vi opray diay lennonia napravlenniay.

B *Na yakorniay*

Yarki ogon vi fonariay biaylago izvetta

2 *Dlia Paroosneegh Soodof*

1 Vseeam paroosneem soodam, idooshtchim na booksiriay eeli pod paroosammi pri priblishennieo igh ki droogomoo Soodnoo, eeli pri priblishennice agtogo loodna ki nim ot zaghoshdiaynia do vosghoshdiaynia solntza veestavliat yarki ogon vi fonar byaylafvo tzviayta tam, gday on lootchschay moshayt biat oosmo

points of each side of the ship, viz., from right a head to 2 points abaft the beam on either side

2 The green light on the starboard side is to be visible in a dark night with a clear atmosphere at a distance of at least 2 miles, and the lantern is to be so constructed as to throw a clear and uninterrupted light over an arc of the horizon of 10 points of the compass, viz, from right a head ' 2 points abaft the beam on the starboard side

3. The red light on the port side must be placed in such a manner as to throw a light in the same way on the port side

4. The side lanterns must be provided with shades or protectors on the inboard side of at least 3 feet in length, so that the colour of them may be seen not otherwise than in the before mentioned directions.

B *At anchor.*

A bright light in the lantern of a white colour.

2 *For Sailing Vessels*

1. On board all sailing vessels, whether being towed or under sail, while approaching any other ship, or being approached by any other vessel, from sunset to sunrise, there shall be placed a bright light in a white lantern in such a place where it can be best seen by the approaching vessel

trayn si priblishayooshtchagossa soodna

2 Vseeam paroosneem soodam stoyashtchim na yakoryay na rayeedagh eeli farvateragh ot zaghoshdiaynia do vosghoshdiaynia solntza eemiayt yarki ogon vi fonarriay bi aylafvo tzviayta na toppiay matchtee za iskhootcheniem tiegh portoff gdiay miaystneemee zakko namee postanovlenniay droogia pravilla otnositelno ognyay na soodagh

3 Fonar podniyattee pri yakarnoi stoyankyee kak na paroghodagh tak i na paroosneegh soodagh shaydooet oostroivat takkeem obrezom tchtobee brosal vokroog yarki i roffnee sweeyait po vsiyaymoo horizontoo.

Obiassnayniay.

Dlia bolshayee yasposti izlagayootsia primyayree iz koigh vidno tcheto pri vsiakoi vstraytchay soo. doff tzviayt vidimeegh ogniay na paroghodiay totchas opray-diay-la,-yet kak naprarleniay tak idiaystviay ki koloromo shay dooyet kash. domoo iz soodoff pristopeet dabee izbiaygnoot stolknovennia

POLOSHAYNIAY 1.

(*See diagram, page 25.*)

Ve aytom poloshayniay paroghod A vidit tolko krasnee ogon na paroghodyay B, vi kotorom bee iz tregh poloshaynee say poshaydnee ninaghodilsyia potomoo tcheto zaylaynice fonar skreet iz vidoo Paroghod A zaklyootcha, et iz etofvo tcheto paroghod B obrashtchenn ki niaymoo hayveem bortom i slaydovatelno proghodit oo nefvo payraid nossom. Po siaymoo yeslee sooda tak bliz ko

2. All sailing vessels at anchor in roadsteads or tideways from sunset to sunrise, must have a clear light in a white lantern on the masthead, excepting in ports, where the local regulations prescribe different rules with regard to ships' lights.

3 The lantern must be hoisted before casting anchor, by steamers as well as by sailing vessels, in such a manner as to cast around a clear and unbroken light over the whole horizon.

Elucidations

For the better illustration, there must be added some examples, from which it may be observed that by every approaching ship, the visible light on board a steamer may be seen in such a direction as to point out what ought to be done by each of the ships, when approaching, so as to avoid collision.

FIRST POSITION.

In this position the steamer A sees only the red light of the steamer B, in whichsoever of the three positions the latter may happen to be, because the green light is hidden from view The steamer A concludes from this that the steamer B turns towards him his port side, and consequently is crossing the bows of A In the same manner, if the vessels are so near to one another as

droogh ki droogoo tcheto mogoot opasatsia stolknoneniа to paroghod A kladayt hayfo roolyia i proghodit tcheesto, Si droogoi storonee parog hod B vi kashdom iz predstavlen, neegh tregh poloshaynnee vidit krasniee i zaylaynice ogni i biaylee ogon na toppiay matchtee paroghoda A raspodoshenniay trayoogolnikom iz tcheto zaklooshchayia tcheto parog-hod A idiaytna niayvo paroghod B mannay-frirooyet kak traybooyet yevo poloshayniay

Ogon na toppiay matchtee vidien vo vseeakom poloshayniay pokka droogoyay Soodno niay ostanniaytsia pozadi traversa

to fear a collision, then the steamer A ports his helm, and passes clear, On the other hand, the steamer B, in either of the said positions, sees the red, green, and masthead lights of the steamer A in a triangular form, from which he concludes that the steamer A approaches towards him, the steamer B manœuvres accordingly.

The light at the top of the mast must be visible in all positions, as long as the second vessel does not pass astern.

POLOSHEYNIAY 2

(See diagram, page 26)

Paroghod A vidya tolko zaylayni ogon paroghoda B moshet yafno zakhootchat tcheto B proghodit oo nefvo pairaid nossom i obrashtchenu ki nyaymoo praveem bortom Si droogoi storonee paroghod B vidya vsay tri ognia paroghoda A moshet zakkhootcheet tcheto paroghod A dyayrshit priyamo nefvo

SECOND POSITION.

The steamer A, seeing only the green light of the steamer B, may easily conclude that the steamer B is before her bow, and turns her starboard side towards her On the other hand, the steamer B, seeing all the three lights of the steamer A, may conclude that the steamer A is steering directly towards her.

POLOSHEYNIAY 3.

(See diagram, page 26.)

Paroghod A i B vzaimno vidiat tolko svoi krasneeay ogni. Zaylaynoeay skreet ot glaz schtcheetammi Oba soodna eedoot obratyas droog ki droogoo lyayveem bottom

THIRD POSITION.

The steamers A and B, mutually seeing only each other's red lights, the green lights being concealed from the eye by the shades, both vessels are passing one another on the port side

POLOSHEYNIAY 4.

(See diagram, page 27.)

Paroghodee A i B veedyat tolko svoi zaylayneeay ogni Krasneeay

FOURTH POSITION.

The steamers A and B see only their green lights, the red lights

zakreetee schtcheetammi Sooda obrashtchaynee droog ki droogoo praveem bortom.

are concealed by the shades, the vessels pass one another to starboard.

POLOSHEYNIAY 5
(See diagram, page 27.)

FIFTH POSITION.

Oda paroghoda vidyat dva tzvetneegh ognia kotoreeay pokazeevayat im tcheto oni eedoot pryammo droog na drooga vi takkom slootchaya oba soodna dolshnee klast lyayvo roolya.

Both steamers see two lights, which shows them that they are approaching towards each other, in such a situation both vessels should put their helm to port

Ob oostroistvyay ognyay.

On Fixing the Lights

Nay obghodimo obrattit osobennoay vnimannyay na sposob ootvershdyayniay tvetneegh ognyayee. Oni dolshnee beat snabshaynnee dyer vyanneemz shtcheetammee si vnodrennyayee storonee dlia tovo tchetobee oba ognya mogli beat vidyeemee vi odno vrayma tolko priyammo si nossa a nyay si droogavo napravlaynva.

It is absolutely necessary that the strictest attention should be paid to the manner of fixing the lights. They ought to be provided with wooden shades, so as to enable both lights to be seen from right a-head, and in no other direction.

Obstoyatteltvo ayto vesma vashno potsmoo tcheto bez aytigh shtchitoff (kotoreeyay vivodyatsya vi pervee ras) nee kakkayay ras polos henniay ogniay niay moshait beet oodorletvoreetyel neem sredstvom dlia ookazannya napravlennia soodna

This is very important, because without the screens (which are now introduced for the first time), any kind of lights would not be effective for the purpose of indicating the direction of the vessels.

Ayto stannoveetsyia sovershenno ponyiatneem pree razomotrennee eezobrashenneegh veeihay tcherty ayshayee eez kotoreegh veedno tcheto vi kakkom bee poloshenny dva soodna nee preebeeshaless droog ki droogoo vi tyeemnot tvetnyay ognee totchas ookas hoot oboim eegh vzaimuoay poloshennee to yest kashdoyay nyeemedlenno ooznayet eedyet lee droogoyay pryammo na nyefvo eelee proghodeet oo nyefvo pairaid nossom ee kotoreem obrashtchenno ki nyemmoo bortom

This will be readily understood by a reference to the above illustrations, from which it will be seen, that in whatever positions two vessels should approach one another in the dark, the coloured light will instantly show to each their relative positions, that is to say, each will know whether the other is approaching directly or crossing the bow, and to which side, either to starboard or port

Critical position not noticed!
— The whole seemingly a translation from English

Ajtovo ookazania sovershenno dostattotchno dlia tovo tchetobee sooda moylee ras ghodeetsya vi samooyoo temnooyoo notch takshay lyegko kak pree dnefnom svyetee ee tolko nyaydostattok takovo ookazania beel preetcheenoyoo mnogeegh nyaytchastneegh slootchayeff

Kashdomoo pryay dostavlyayetsa oopotroblyat fonarree takovo roda kakkeeyay boodoot naedyeneeoodob nyay ishemee si tyem odnakkoshay tchetobee veeshayeezloshenneeya ooslovya beetee vi tchetobee fonarree vpolnyae so otvets tvovalee predpoloshennoi tzvaylee

These regulations are fully calculated to enable vessels to pass each other in the darkest night, as if in clear daylight, and will only be found deficient by parties not observing them

It is left to every one to use in preference any description of lantern he may see fit, with this exception only, that they shall answer the above conditions, and be provided with proper lights.

SWEDEN.

1852   No 41
Swensk—Författnings—Samling
(*Upplases fran Predikstolen*)
Kongl Maj ts Nadiga Forordning anguende de lanternor, hwarmed, till undwikande af ombordlaggning, såwäl ångfartyg i allmanhet, som de seglande fartyg, hwilka begagnas i saltsjon eller u frammande farwatten bora wara forsedde

Gifven Stockholms Slott,
    den 25 Augusti, 1852
Wi, Oscar, med Guds nåde, Sweriges, Noriges, &c., Konung, gore weterligt, att sedan Kongl. Storbritanniska Regeringen hos Osz framstallt den onskan, att Swenska fartyg matte erhalla foreskrift att, till undwikande af ombordlaggning under natt och morker, anwanda det for Storbritanniska fartyg anbefallda satt att for hwarandra tillkannagifwa sitt

1852   No. 41
Collection of Swedish Ordinances
Published from the pulpit.
His Royal Majesty's gracious ordinance respecting the lanterns with which, for the purpose of avoiding collision, both steam vessels in general and sailing vessels, which may be met with at sea or in foreign waters, are required to be supplied

Given at the Palace of Stockholm,
    25th August, 1852.
We, Oscar, by the grace of God King of Sweden, Norway, &c., make known that the Royal Government of Great Britain having expressed to Us the desire that Swedish vessels should, for the purpose of avoiding collisions during the night, or darkness, be required to observe the regulations established for the vessels of Great Britain for the purpose of

låge, nemligen medelst lanternor, lysande med dels kulört, dels hwitt sken, hafwe Wi efter inhemtande af war forwaltnings af sjöurendena underdåniga utlåtande i ämnet funnit godt att, med ändring, hwad ångfartyg särskilt angär, af hwad genom § 15 i War nådiga förordning den 1 November, 1849 stadgats i afseende på passagerareångfartygs förseende med lanternor till efterrättelse från och med den 1 nästkommande Januari i näder förordna följande

1 Alla Swenska ångfartyg skola till sjös, å redder, floder och kanaler, samt i hamnar och wikar, från solens nedgång till desz uppgång, föra lanternor af nedannämnde bestaffenhet och på efterföljande satt nämligen

Under Gaeng.

En lanterna med hwitt sken på förtoppen

En dito med grönt sken på styrbordsidan

En dito med rödt sken på babordsidan

Topplanternan, som bör kunna synas på ett afstånd af minst fem minuter i mörk natt med klar luft, skall wara så inrättad, att den wisar ett likformigt och stadigt sken öfwer en båge å horizonten af tjugu kompass streck, eller tio streck på hwarje sida af fartyget, nämligen för-ifrån till twå streck akter om twars

Sid lanternorna med kulört sken som i mörk natt med klar luft böra kunna synas på ett afstånd af minst twå minuter, skola wara så inrättade, att de wisa ett likformigt oct stadigt

making known their position, viz, by means of lanterns, some with coloured and some with white lights. We have, after previous consideration of a memorial on the subject, submitted by our Board of Maritime Affairs, seen fit to alter, as far as concerns steamers in particular, the stipulations contained in § 15 of our gracious ordinance of 16th November, 1849, regarding the furnishing of passenger steamers with lanterns, and to issue the following order, to be observed from and after the 1st of January next.

All Swedish Steam Vessels shall, when at sea, or in roadsteads, harbours, and canals, as also in bays and rivers, from the setting of the sun till its rising, carry lanterns of the description mentioned below, and in the following manner

When in Motion

A lantern with a white light at the foremast head.

One with a green light on the starboard side

One with a red light on the larboard side.

The masthead light, which must be visible at a distance of at least five miles in a dark night with a clear atmosphere, and the lantern is to be so arranged as to show a uniform and steady light over an arc of the horizon of twenty points of the compass, being ten points on each side of the ship, viz, from right ahead to two points abaft the beam. The side lanterns with coloured lights such as in a dark night with a clear atmosphere can be seen at a distance of at least two miles, are to be so

M

sken, omfattande hwardera en båge å horizonten af tio kompasz-streck, nämligen för ifrån till twå streck akter-om twärs, den gröna på styrbords och den röda på babordsidan.

Å innersidan af sid lanternorna skola deszutom anbringas skärmar, minst tre fot långa, för att hindra deras sken att korsaas för ombogen.

Till Ankars.

En lanterna med wanligt klart sken.

2. Alla seglande fartyg, hwilka begagnas i saltsjön eller i främmande farwatten, skola då de, mellan solens nedgång och desz uppgång, till segels eller under bogsering nalkas annat fartyg wisa en lanterna med klart sken på sådant sätt, att det bäst kan bemärkas af det andra fartyget, och i så god tid att ombordläggning kan undwikas.

Dylika seglande fartyg skola likaledes, då de ligga till ankars å redder eller der fartyg paszera, från solens nedgång till desz uppgång, hafwa å masttoppen hiszad en lanterna med ett stadigt klart sken, utom i hamnar eller å sådane ställer der andra föreskrifter i afseende å lanterna för fartyg äro lagligen gällande.

3. De lanternor som begagnas till ankars, både af ångfartyg och af seglande fartyg, böra wara så inrättade, att de wisa ett klart och starkt sken omkring hela horizonten.

4. Det är wederbörande öppet lemnadt, att förse sig med hwad slags lanternor som helst, såwida endast

constructed as to show a similar uniform and steady light, each spanning an arc of the horizon of ten points of the compass, viz., from right ahead to two points abaft the beam, the green light on the starboard side and the red on the larboard side.

On the inner side of the side lights there shall moreover be fitted screens of at least three feet long to prevent the lights from being seen across the bow.

When at Anchor.

A lantern with a common bright light.

All Sailing Vessels which frequent the seas or foreign waters shall, from the setting of the sun to its rising, when under sail or being towed, and approaching another vessel, show a lantern with a bright light in such manner that it may be best observed by the other vessel, and also in such good time as to avoid collision.

In the same manner Sailing Vessels, when they lie at anchor in roadsteads or fairways, shall, from sunset till sunrise, have hoisted at the masthead a lantern with a constant bright light, except within harbours or other places where other regulations respecting lights for ships are legally established.

The lantern to be used when at anchor, both by steam vessels and sailing vessels, is to be so constructed as to show a clear good light all round the horizon.

It is left to all concerned to furnish themselves with whatever kind of lantern they prefer, so that all

alla har ofwan meddelade föreskrifte behörigen iakttagas.

De till förtydligande af ifrågawarande signaleringssatt erforderliga ritningar och närmare underrattelser komma, att genom Wårt och Rikets Commerce Collegii försorg wederborande meddelas

Det alle, som wederbor, hafwe sig horsamligen att efterralta Till yttermarmurszo hafwe Wi detta nud egen hand underskrifwit och med Wart Kongl. Sigill bekrafta latit

STOCKHOLM SLOTT,
den 25 Augusti, 1852.

(L.S.)

Under Hans Majts Wår Allenadigste Konungs och Herres frånwaro
Sweriges och Norriges Interimo-Regering,

G. A. SPARRE, FREDR. DUC,
STGERNALA, C O. PALMSTJERNA
I. F FÅHRÆAS, C. HOHENHAUSER,
Foredragande
N F WALLENSTEIN, CARL G. MORNER,
C H. ULNER, H. REUTERDAHL,
&c. &c.

1852. No 49.
SWENSK.—FORFATTNINGS—SAMLING.
Kongl Majts och Rikets Commerce-Collegii Cirkular till Magistraterne i Rikets Sjö-och Stapelstader angaende närmare underrattelser till fortydligande af det for öng fartyg i nåder foreskifna signal eriingssatt medelst lanternor

Utfardadt i Stockholm,
Der 29 Sept , 1852

the regulations above laid down be properly observed.

The drawings and more minute instructions necessary to explain the system of signals in question will be communicated to those whom it may concern, through our College of Commerce.

To which all concerned are commanded to render due obedience In further confirmation, we have subscribed this decree with our own hand, and caused it to be sealed with our royal seal.

PALACE OF STOCKHOLM,
Aug 22, 1852.

(L.S.)

During the absence of H M our most gracious King and Lord,
The interim Regency of Sweden and Norway,

G A SPARRE, FRED DUC,
&c., &c.

On the proposition of
N. F. WALLENSTEIN, C G. MORNER, &c &c.

1852. No. 49.
COLLECTION OF SWEDISH ORDINANCES
The Circular of the Royal and National College of Commerce to the Magistrates of the Sea and Staple Towns concerning more accurate information to explain the mode of Signals by means of Lanterns prescribed for steam vessels

Published at Stockholm,
29 Sept , 1852.

Sedan Kongl Maj:ts. under den 25 sistlidne Augusti utfärdat nådig forordning angående de lanternor hwarmed till undwikande af ombordläggning, så wäl ångfartyg i allmänhet, som de seglande fartyg, hwilka begagnas i salsjon eller å främmande farwatten böra från och med den 1 Jan, 1853, wara försedda, har Kongl Collegium skolat Magistraten till wederbörandes förständigande harigenom meddela följande till fortydligande af det sålunda i nåder anbefallda signaleringssättet Kongl Collegium delgifna närmare underrättelser och ritningar å ångfartygens olika ställningar till hwar andra, nemligen

Since H M. the King, under date of the 25th of August last, issued a gracious ordinance respecting the Lanterns with which for the purpose of avoiding collision, both steam vessels in general and sailing vessels, which meet either in our own or foreign waters, must be supplied, from and after the 1st January, 1853 The Royal College hereby has to communicate to the Magistrates for the parties concerned, the following particulars and sketches respecting the different positions of steamers towards each other, which have been furnished the Royal College, in explanation of the mode of signalling so established, viz

Första Ställningen

First Situation

(See diagram, page 25.)

Har ser ångfartyget A endast den röda lanternan på fartyget B, i hwilken position af de tre här angifna det sednare och må wara, tyden gröna lanternan forblifwer skymd Fartyget A finner fartyget B's babordssida emot sig och att således det sednare passerar forom fartyget A babord kan Fartyget A girar derföre om fartygen äro hwarandra så nära att fara är for ombordläggning styrbord han och går klart Fartyget B, åter ser i hwarje af de tre positionerna den röda den gröna och topplanternan å fartyget A i en triangulär form hwaraf fartyget B finner fartyget A styra rakt emot sig och rättar sin manöver derefter

Here the steamer A only sees the red lantern on board the vessel B, in whichsoever position of the three here represented the last may be, since the green lantern remains hidden The vessel A finds B's port side towards him, and so that the last can pass ahead of the vessel A to port. The vessel A therefore, if so near that there is danger of collision, will port his helm and go clear

But the other vessel, B, in any one of the three positions, sees the red, the green, and the masthead lanterns on board the vessel A in a triangular form, by which the vessel B will know that the vessel A is steering directly towards him, and regulates his manœuvres accordingly

Andra Ställningen.
(See diagram, page 26.)

Här är endast den gröna lanternan på fartyget B synlig för fartyget A som deraf tydligen finner att B paszerar för om detsamma styrbord han Då de tre lanternorna på fartyget A synas, finner fartyget B förstnämnda fartyg styra rakt emog sig

Second Situation
(See diagram, page 26.)

Here the green lantern of the vessel B only is visible to the vessel A, which perceives in time that B is crossing to starboard Since the three lanterns of the vessel A are visible, the vessel B perceives that the first-named vessel is steering directly towards him

Tredje Ställningen
(See diagram, page 26.)

Fartygen A och B se endast hvarandras röda lanternor. De gröna skymmas af skärmarne. Båda fartygen paszera hwarandra om babord

Third Situation
(See diagram, page 26.)

The vessels A and B only see each other's red lanterns The green ones are hidden by the screens Both vessels will pass one another to port.

Fjerde Ställningen
(See diagram, page 27.)

Här är endast den gröna lanternan synlig för hwardera fartyget A och B. De röda skymmas af skärmarna. Fartygen paszera alltså hwarandra om styrbord

Fourth Situation.
(See diagram, page 27.)

Here the green lantern only is visible to each vessel A and B The red ones are hidden by the screens The vessels will therefore pass one another to starboard

Femte Ställningen.
(See diagram, page 27.)

De bägge fargade skenen synliga för hwardera fartyget utwisa att deszä styra rakt emot hwarandra. Båda böra da gira styrbord han

Fifth Situation.
(See diagram, page 27.)

Both the coloured lights being visible to each vessel point out that they are steering direct towards each other Both must in this case put their helms to port

Stockholm, den 29 Sept., 1852
Pa Konigl Majts. och Rikets,
Commerce Collegii Wägnar
C. D SKOGMAN.

T. WILLERDING

Stockholm, 29th Sept., 1852
Royal and National Commercial College
C D SKOGMAN

T WILLERDING

INDEX.

A

ACCIDENT, 100
ADMIRALTY Court, 4. 40.
    ,,   Regulations of 1848, 1852, 21.
AGROUND, vessel, collision, 96.
AMERICAN regulations, 140
ANCHOR, vessel at, collision, 80.
    manner, 84, 85 87
    parting from, 82
    single anchor, 87.
    suddenly, 84 89
    responsibility, 82
  Lights, 22
    not formerly generally required, 5, 6
    under present regulations, 74.
    approaching, 117. 121, 122
APPROACHING, direct, both port, 27
AVOID, collision, duty of both vessels if possible, 84 86. 100. 104.

B

BRITISH subject, action against a foreigner, 66, 67
    ,,   waters, 68
BOWSPRIT, lantern at, not according to regulations, 60
BURNING of lights, attention to be paid to, 29 33 39, 40, 41

C.

CLOSE-HAULED, 97
COLLISION, one vessel at rest, 80
    different tacks, 97
    one free, 101.
    both free, 107
    possibilities, vis major,
    both vessels in fault,
    fault of one party,
    that party suffering,
    party, *Woodrop* v *Sims*, 2 Dod 85,
    on the high seas, 65
COLOURED lights, 39 76.
COMMITTEE on subject of lights, 15. 75.
COMMAND, under, 123 126
COSTS, security in case of foreigners, 67
    independent of value of ship,
    Dundee, 2 Hag. 137.
    John Dunn, 8 M. S M 262
    condemnation in,
    on account of inhumanity, 102.
CROSS ACTION, 43.
CUSTOM, superseded by Admiralty regulations, 126.
    Friends, 2 Ca 100.
    Sylph, 2 Sp 80.

D

DAMAGE, division, both parties in fault, effect, 8
    as against owner, limited to value of ship and freight, 3 Hag 433
    value of ship, &c , just before collision, *Benares*, 7 Ca 51
DANGER, immediate, 123. 125.

DANISH regulations, 140
DIAGRAM, in illustration, 25
DIFFERENT TACKS, vessels on, 97
DISTANCE, 85 125.
DOCKS, collision, 91.
DRAGGING, 88
DREDGING, 97
DRIFTING, 88, 89

E

END-ON, 122.
EXCEPTIONS, 104.

F.

FAIRWAY, 23. 93. 115.
FISHING SMACK, collision, 33. 92. 96
FOG-HORN, 77.
FOREIGNER, right to sue in British court, 65.
    costs, give security, 67
FOREIGN VESSEL, collision with British, 66 68. 71, 72.
    collision with another foreign vessel, 66. 69 71.
    on the high seas, 62 64
    in British waters, 62, 63 70, 71.
    regulations, effect on, 70
FOUL BERTH, 88, 89 91.
FREE, one vessel, 101.
    both, 79 107
FRENCH regulations, 135

G

GIVING WAY, getting out of way, *Gazelle*, 5 Ca 103
GREEN LIGHT on starboard bow of steamer, 22.
    only visible, 121 124, 125

H.

HAILING, 89
HARBOUR, collision in, 81
HOISTING light, 60. 115
HOLLAND regulations, 142.
HOVE-TO, 93 101

I.

INABILITY to avoid, 81
INEVITABLE accident, 35 84. 98 101 107.

J.

JURISDICTION, extent, 64, 65. 73

L

LAID-TO, 45
LANTERN, capacity, 40

LANTERN—*continued.*
    description, 22 115
    insufficiency, 61.
LARBOARD TACK, 79
LEX LOCI, 71, 72
LIEN, after collision, none, *Abbot*, 533
    Chimera, Nov 22, 1852.
LIGHTS, ancient law, 2
    circumstances may require, 51
    authority to regulate conferred on the Lords of Admiralty, 15.
    coloured, 14
    description, 22. 115
    efficiency, 22 74 76
    fixed, 27 76
    hoisted, 9 44 115
    going out, 31 41
    position, 76 114.
    masthead, 22
    present law, 68
    signal for pilots, 4 76
    showing, 9, 10. 35. 37, 38
    steamers, 29 75
    regulations of 1848, 22
    regulations of 1852, 21
LOCAL REGULATIONS, *vide* Custom, 126.
LOOK-OUT, 66 77
LORDS OF THE ADMIRALTY, power respecting regulations, 15. 116.
LYING-ASHORE, 90
LYING-TO, 91, 92. 121

M

MASTERS, penalty for neglect of regulations, 23
    wilful default, when so considered, 24
MASTHEAD, light at, 22 30

MASTHEAD—*continued*
    very top, 30.
    not exhibited there, 32. 35. 45 51 53 116.
MECKLENBERG, 143
MEETING, 105 117 119, 120
MERCHANT SHIPPING ACT, 15 17 29
    § 296, 72
MERCHANT SHIPPING REPEAL ACT, 20.
MISSING STAYS, collision, 95. 101.
MOORED, collision, 86. 90.
MOTIONLESS, 80

N.

NARROW CHANNEL, 112, 126
NIGHT, kind of, 58. 107.
    vessel on different tacks meeting at, 99 106

O.

OCCASIONED, accident, by neglect of rules 116 and 127, 32 42.
    46 48, 49, 50, 51, 52, 53, 54, 55 57, 58 60.
    not so, 43, 44, 45, 46, 47 49. 52. 56.

P

PAY OFF, 95
PAYING OUT CABLE, 83.
PENALTY, effect of, 116.
PILOT, if compulsory, and he solely in fault, owners exonerated
    (Merchant Shipping Act, § 388, *Abbot*, 158), 66 87 89
    not if crew also to blame, *Ripon*, 6 Ca 252,

PILOT—*continued*
    also *Hape*, June 23, 1854,
    see also *Duke of Sussex*, 1 Ca. 164, *Lucy* v *Ingram*, there cited,
    and *Eden*, 4 Ca. 469,
PRESUMPTION, 33.
PROOF, affirmative, presumption in favour of, 97.
    burden of, 40 104 107.
    lights, 31 36, 37.
    presumptive, 33.
    want of, 107.
PRUSSIAN regulations, 144.
PUTTING ABOUT, 94, 95.

R

RECOVERY, loss of right, 116 122
RED LIGHT, port side of steamer, 22
REEFING, collision, 92, 93 101.
REGULATIONS of 1848, 14. 21.
    of 1852, under 14 & 15 Vic., c. 79, 21. 75.
    in force after repeal of that statute, 15, 61.
    previous, revoked by those of 1852, 23.
    violation, penalty, 93.
    violation, noticed by Court, 49. 52, 53.
REPORT on lights, 14, 15.
REST, vessel at, collision, 79.
ROAD, rule of, 79.
ROADSTEAD, 23 51.
RUDDER, detached, 96.
RULES, application, 98

S

SAILS, management of, 83. 89. 92 95 100
SAILING vessels to show lights, 75, 76
    at anchor, at masthead, 23
SCREENS, 23 27. 75, 76.
SHOWING LIGHTS, 59.
STARBOARD TACK 79.
STATUTES, application, 118, 119.
STATUTES, 6 Geo. 4, c. 125....72.
    9 & 10 V., c 100....13. 21. 29. 76. 110
    § 10......16
    § 11, 12 . 17.
    § 13......19 112
    14 & 15 V , c 79.... 29 61
    § 16....25. 26
    § 27....111
    § 28....18. 42. 112.
    repealed, 20.
    17 & 18 V., c. 104 (Merchant Shipping Act), 15, 16.
    § 293....72
    § 297....126.
    § 295....16
    § 296....16 18. 70. 111. 120.
    § 298....16 70. 93 112
    § 299....16. 19. 113
    17 & 18 V., c. 120 (Merchant Shipping Repeal Act), 20.
    § 4......7. 61.
STAYS, 94, 95.
    in missing, 95. 101.
STEAMERS' LIGHTS, under steam, 22.
    at anchor, 23
    free, 109
    Birkenhead, 6 Ca 369.
SPEED, 8. 17 85.

STEAM-TUG, non-responsibility of, when towing.
    Duke of Sussex, 1 Ca. 165.
    Hope, June 23, 1854
STEAM WHISTLE, 77
SWEDEN, 152

T

TACKS, different, collision, 79.
TACKING, collision, 93, 94.
TIME, vessel ought to act in sufficient, 11, 12 34 94. 102. 106 108.
    ought to wear in sufficient, 11 100.
TOWING, vessel towed responsible v. Steam Tug
TRAWLS, vessel lying at, 56 96.
TRINITY HOUSE REGULATIONS, 108.

V

VALUE, *vide* Costs and damage, Abbot, 300
VESSEL, condition of, 125.

W

WEATHER, 12
WILFUL DEFAULT, 24.

Y.

YARDS, sending down, 89

CPSIA information can be obtained at www.ICGtesting.com
229318LV00004B/122/P